THE
CARS
IN MY LIFE

Le Mans 1927. W.O. standing beside one of his
3-litres. George Duller is at the wheel

W. O. BENTLEY

THE
CARS
IN MY LIFE

THE MACMILLAN COMPANY
NEW YORK
1963

First Published in The United States of
America by The Macmillan Company,
1963

By the same author

'W.O.' AN AUTOBIOGRAPHY

A PATHFINDER BOOK REPRINT EDITION
Complete and Unabridged

Printed in the United States of America

ISBN: 979-8-8691-7097-2

Printed in Great Britain

CONTENTS

ILLUSTRATIONS

THE
CARS
IN MY LIFE

I

The Cars in My Life

A FEW years ago I published my autobiography, which was interesting to write[1] and was kindly received. It was not a long book and was more an account of the things that had happened to me and the story of the projects and companies with which I have been associated than a personal autobiography. This book is not an elaboration of the earlier one, nor is it (heaven forbid!) more personal in any sense of that term. It is, if you like, a book of theories and opinions, a hotch-potch of ideas on motor cars, motoring and the motor industry—and a few other things besides. I also say something about the cars I have known, some of the cars for which I was responsible and even some of the cars which never came to anything. Stirred into the stew as spice are a few theories, for what they are worth, on the principle of motor-car design and something about the people I have known in the world of motoring.

I don't pretend for a moment that any of this is very important; but while I still have the energy and the memory to do so, I thought it might be amusing to pass on these thoughts, if only for their entertainment value. Some may be positively valuable, others may be taken as lessons which I learnt and from which benefit may be gained by others.

---

[1] Like this book, it was in fact 'ghosted' by Richard Hough, who prepared the text from my notes and from information I gave him in the course of numerous talks we had together at Shamley Green.

[11]

There are no lessons to be learnt from this first chapter, which is the only one that qualifies for inclusion at all under the title I have given the book. It is about the motor cars I have owned or driven extensively over the years. Some of them bore my name, most did not.

Like everything else in this book, what I have to say is essentially personal, and is full of the foibles and prejudices as well as the opinions of one who has spent half his life in a driving seat. A driver's choice of motor car and his likes and dislikes are essentially personal things anyway, just as a man's car is often taken to reflect the character of the individual. There is no use in making sweeping generalizations, and I have often said that no one should tell anyone else what sort of motor car to buy; it nearly always leads to tears and lost friends.

I have been prevailed upon to open on this subject because I am told that people love to read about the cars of others. Here, then, are some of mine.

I started off with a Riley, a water-cooled V-twin of 86 × 89 mm with the engine under the seat and placed centrally. Like the Grand Prix cars of today, it was neither a rear- nor a front-engined vehicle; but, unlike those successful machines, it did not hold the road very well, and with its wheelbase of 6 ft. 6 in. was a terrible skidder. The 'dreaded side-slip' which was the subject of such awesome conversation in those days occurred very frequently. It was quite a good little performer and accelerated forwards with an alacrity equalled only by its accleration backwards, the latter being usually unpremeditated. It was, of course, chain-driven and, as was usual in those days, one was quite open to the elements. I wasn't really sorry to see it go.

At this time—around 1910—my main interest was tending to stray from locomotives to the motor car and I was fascinated by French machines. The Unic taxi, for example, was a prosaic-enough vehicle in all conscience, but I acquired a tremendous respect for Unics during the months I spent with the National Motor Cab Company.

They were very strongly built, with twin-cylinder engines, and very reliable. Nothing the English built at the time could stand up to the treatment nor show such economical running figures.

The practical, common-sense streak in the French character, which tends to be overlooked by foreigners (especially Americans and Britons who sometimes feel the French are decadent and 'finished'), has always been reflected in their motor cars. The Unic was a down-to-earth machine which did the job for which it was intended. All these remarks applied also to my own first real car, which I bought because of my admiration for French engineering. This was a Sizaire-Naudin, a two-seater single-cylinder machine which was advanced in some respects, merely curious in others and thoroughly practical all through. It had a single-cylinder engine of 120×130 mm capacity which was astonishingly reliable and economical. Also, it always started—an unusual advantage at that time. Some forty years before a British manufacturer included such a refinement it had independent front suspension, on the sliding-column principle similar to that adopted by Lancia and Morgan in the 'twenties, with a transverse leaf spring. All this was very simple and effective and provided astonishingly good road-holding, although this could have been further improved if the manufacturer had not insisted on placing the gearbox in the back axle, which unnecessarily increased the unsprung weight. The Sizaire, incidentally, had quite a sporty reputation at this time and the car did very well in competition, especially the voitwette racing. I believe that a small Sizaire, driven by Naudin himself, won a sort of voiturette Targa Florio run on the Targa circuit in about 1906.

This single-cylinder Sizaire was followed by a four-cylinder car of the same make which I bought from the concessionaires, Jarrott and Letts, second-hand. This was a good car, too, but not nearly so satisfactory as the first one. Its four-stroke, four-cylinder, water-cooled engine was not quite so reliable, and it had a very noisy camshaft. But of course it was much faster than the earlier machine.

After I had had the second Sizaire for some months, my brother H.M. and I acquired the concession for the French D.F.P. or Doriot, Flandrin et Parant, and at the same time I said a rather regretful farewell to the steady old Unic taxis. From the machines that were in stock I took over a two-seater coupé 12/15. All the same, D.F.P.s were excellent, reliable vehicles possessing the indefinable quality that makes certain cars a pleasure to drive, and always feel 'just right'. The steering and road-holding were first class and they were ruggedly built to stand up to the very harsh treatment all Frenchmen give their cars.

By this time I was becoming interested in the sheer performance of motor cars, and felt drawn towards what we used to call 'speed work'. Hill-climbs and sprints appealed to me and I was anxious to acquire a vehicle that would be suitable for Brooklands, on which I had occasionally raced my motor bicycles in the past. I soon became tremendously enthusiastic about the D.F.P. and felt that it had real tuning potential. So in due course we put up the compression ratio on my own 12/15 and carried out various other modifications to the breathing and exhaust system, all of which made it quite a fast little motor car. Later, the modifications which I carried out to my guinea pig were applied at the Paris works to some of the 12/15 cars we imported from France, which, as the 12/40, began to acquire quite a sporty reputation. I have told in my autobiography how we fitted aluminium pistons and surprised quite a number of people as a result. The standard 12/40, for example, managed a very comfortable 60 m.p.h. even with a heavy saloon body and was a match for almost anything you were likely to meet on the road at that time.

We imported the D.F.P.s in chassis form from France and the bodies were supplied to the customers' specifications, but we also had standard bodywork which J. H. Easter of New Street Mews, near Baker Street Station, used to build. When I look back on the materials we used and the care and atten-

The start of it all: the 3-litre prototype ready for road test
in 1921

Preparing the special-bodied 3-litre for the record attempt at Montlhery
in 1926. The rear of our Bullnose Morris Cowley is on the right

Leroux does some last-minute checking on the 12/50 D.F.P. at
Brooklands in 1914 while I look on

D.F.P. at Shelsley Walsh

tion that were given to the trim and bodywork on each chassis I realize that these could be matched today only by the one or two surviving specialist coachbuilders. The 12/15 D.F.P. used to sell with four-seater enclosed coachwork for £385 in 1914, the 12/40 Sports for £410, but for this money the customer had absolutely top-quality West of England cloth upholstery, tailor-made especially for the car. The panel-beating was done by hand, of course, and the wooden framework and trim were made by real craftsmen carpenters who were dedicated to their calling. The painting took literally weeks, and each of the coats was hand-smoothed down after brushing and finished off with several coats of varnish. (In spite of all this attention, such has been the advance in the standards of materials for painting cars that I wouldn't change the cellulose finish on my cheap mass-produced car today for that which we used on the D.F.P.)

Incidentally, at New Street we had a wonderful old character who used to paint the fine decorative lines on the coachwork which were a *sine qua non* on any vehicle at that time. He was never, in my memory, anything but very drunk indeed, but with the aid of a supporting stick he painted the most beautiful fine lines with complete confidence and never the trace of a waver.

That renowned motor the Rolls-Royce Silver Ghost was another car of the immediate pre-war period with which I had a good deal of experience as a friend of mine owned one. At £998 without bodywork it was a very expensive car, even for those days. It may sound rather trite, but since I am making comments on the cars I know about I will have to say that its most lasting impression was its silence. I suppose by the standards of today this was not the thing that would strike you first, and it might even sound rather noisy beside a cheap modern V8 American car, but in 1912 the outstanding feature of almost every motor car was its noise: the noise from the exhaust, rear axle, gearbox, tappets and everything else. The other thing that struck you about the Ghost as soon as you started off was the smoothness of the pick-up, when clutches were chancy things indeed, and the absence of vibration. It was also marvellously reliable, of course, and the controls worked beautifully and the detail finish was of the highest standard.

The astonishing silence of the Silver Ghost could be broken only when you pulled a little lever, clearly marked 'Not to be used in Great Britain', which operated a cut-out, caused a very satisfactory sound from the exhaust and provided a fractional increase in power, with an increase in top speed of a few m.p.h. To drive a Silver Ghost at walking speed with the cut-out open was one of the minor pleasures in life for me at that time.

I must just mention Dunhills of Euston Road while we are in this nostalgic vein. They make pipes now, of course, but at that time Dunhills was the natural gathering point for all motor enthusiasts, who would make the trek to N.W.1 for their clothing and accessories. At Dunhills you could get superlative brass horns, and lamps, special windscreens and hoods and every other form of accessory. They also sold those huge, long, fur coats which were so essential for open driving in winter, gloves and veils of all kinds, special motoring luggage and, what I remember most vividly, the Dunhill coat with rubber neck and heavily proofed material held together by great clips which went right down to the calves. And very essential this was, too.

While my brother and I had the D.F.P. concession I made it my business to drive all the models and, particularly in the last year before the 1914 war, I did quite a lot of competition work and record-breaking in tuned D.F.P.s with special bodywork. I enjoyed this, of course, but the principal objective was to demonstrate the car's potential and improve sales. Even in its standard form the 12/40 was quite a fast car for its time and I would often go up to Coventry from London in under two hours, a time which would be quite difficult today, even with the assistance of M1. This was during the war when I was working at the Admiralty, and I made the trip so frequently, and with rather less care for the engine than I should have done, that I eventually put a con. rod through the crankcase at Stony Stratford. That this did not happen before was a remarkable tribute to the durability of that fine old car.

The only D.F.P. that wasn't very good was the big 16/20 which we imported in very small numbers. At one time I had a fixed-head coupé, but did not like it so much as the 12/40. It had a very high centre of gravity and the engine, with its weak crankshaft, very long stroke and tendency to vibrate, was not nearly so satisfactory. I kept my nice old 12/40 saloon until the first 3-litre Bentley came off the production line.

Another car I ran during the 1914–18 war was an open, four-seater Cadillac V8 which I bought after I damaged my D.F.P. This was a very remarkable machine in many ways. It had a huge wooden steering wheel, and was very expensive on petrol at a time when this was rather scarce, although as I was working for a Government department this should not have unduly worried me. The Cadillac was one of the most flexible cars in top gear that I have ever driven and was astonishingly quiet. While some firms today boast that the passengers in their cars can hear only the clock at 100 m.p.h., the only mechanical sound from a Cadillac at a very creditable top speed was its fan. I used to love to take it to Derby and, starting in top gear, drive it at a slow walking pace round the Rolls-Royce works to show off its flexibility. This was really only a leg-pull, but it used to exasperate those present.

The engine dimensions were 79 × 130 mm, giving a capacity of 5100 c.c., and it was, I believe, among the first V8s the Americans produced. The widely spaced three-speed gearbox was in unit with the engine, which was 'three-point suspended', forward by a ball-and-socket bearing. It had a three-bearing crankshaft, and a single central camshaft with eight cams, each operating two valves. Tungsten steel exhaust valves and tulip-shaped inlet valves were other interesting features, as was the two-cylinder tyre pump fitted at the front end of the dynamotor shaft, which included an oil-separating chamber 'to prevent oil being carried into the tyres with air'—a sensible-enough precaution.

To drive in the Cadillac alone with the hood down was a strange sensation rather like navigating an empty barge along a canal. Its body was truly vast and with let-down seats that increased the passenger capacity to seven. The detail work and standards of bodywork finish did not perhaps quite match its mechanical refinement, but the Cadillac did have its merits and I sold it at a very satisfactory profit.

Many years later, when I was with Rolls-Royce, I often drove another Cadillac owned by the company and used for experimental purposes. This was a V16 of such mammoth dimensions that it would have dwarfed even that earlier American car. My chief memories of this automobile (although that term is inadequate) were its astonishing refinement with perhaps the most completely successful elimination of evidence that explosions were occurring under the bonnet ever obtained in a motor car. The word 'torque' also took on a new meaning with this V16, which could reach 90 m.p.h. with a sort of endless limousine body of goodness knows what weight. Finally—and one could never get away from this—there was the impression of sheer size this car has left; and of attempting, like the captain of the *Queen Mary* docking during a tugboat strike, to manœuvre this Cadillac through the gates of Hyde Park and into the dock basin of Marble Arch.

I don't think many English people can have driven the American Franklin of the 1914–18 era, and it may surprise some to learn that the Corvair is not the first production, air-cooled six-cylinder car to be built in America.

In fact, Franklin were producing six-cylinder air-cooled engines as long ago as 1905, and an advertisement for that car asked: 'How does "Franklin Air-Cooling" make a more powerful engine, and an abler car for less money?' and answered its own question: 'By creating a more efficient temperature in the combustion chambers than is possible in any other engine. By also getting rid of weight. By saving repair cost and weight cost, and by giving more day's work in a year.' Good sense, too!

The Franklin, which belonged to 'E' Section of the Admiralty and which I drove for many miles during the first war, was a very pleasant motor, though its performance was negligible considering the size of its engine. It was also, I believe, very expensive for its time. It was cooled by a huge fan set in the flywheel, which drew air between the fine vertical cooling fins and the cylinders of sheet metal round the cylinders themselves. This cooling system was completely satisfactory and must have been a great advantage in the northern United States in winter weather. But the fan moaned rather, as it tends to do on all air-cooled cars, though why no one has got round this problem I cannot imagine. The Franklin had overhead valves operated by push rods and it had a wooden frame with huge full elliptic springs fore and aft.

One car I drove quite often in France during the Bentley Motors period was the eight-cylinder, Knight sleeve-valve Panhard, a very representative French motor car, reliable and tough. This one was fitted with a very rakish two-seater body, and from the driving seat the radiator cap appeared almost as a dot on the horizon. It was astonishingly fast, and the car's owner thought nothing of running down to Cannes from Paris without a night stop. The suspension especially was far ahead of anything we had then, and this superiority applies as strongly today. The French are blessed by some poorly surfaced main roads and abominably bad second-class roads. As a result, they have always had the best suspension on their cars of any nation. British designers have unhappily been cursed with beautifully surfaced main roads for many years, although I do think it is high time we recognized the fact that some of our cars are exported to countries which have main roads little better than cart-tracks.

I have lapped Montlhery in several high-performance cars,

including a 3-litre Bentley at 105 m.p.h., but I wonder if anyone else has been round Montlhery in a bull-nose Morris Cowley at 48 m.p.h.? This took some doing. But what an admirable little vehicle that Morris was! The Company Cowley was one of those pretty short-chassis occasional four-seater tourers, and was used at Montlhery for transporting the mechanics to and from the hotel and the track during our 1926 record-breaking.

The Cowley, with its sturdy Hotchkiss-built engine, was very reliable and had no vices. It also had a most endearing starter, which everyone who has driven one will remember. This was done in complete silence, without any engagement of noisy pinions, with a dynamotor, which also acted, through a different gear, as a dynamo for the other electrics. It was eventually dropped by Lucas because it was rather heavy and expensive to make, and also there was sometimes trouble when the engine backfired. I thought provision could have been made for this contingency and later tried to persuade Lucas to develop it, but they weren't interested.

During the Bentley Motors period I know I should have driven other people's cars far more than I did, but it was a hectic time between 1919 and 1931 for all of us, and all my time, energy and resources were so single-mindedly devoted to our own cars that I very rarely drove any others.

But I cannot begin to calculate the mileage I covered in the various Bentleys. The car I think I shall always remember best in my motoring life was the 8-litre, which I had fitted into a $6\frac{1}{2}$-litre chassis with a very pleasant, if abominably square and ugly, Weymann fabric body.

What a blessing those Weymann bodies were! When metal coachbuilding resulted in a continuous and ever-varying chorus of rattles and squeaks and chirrups, and a weight that terribly handicapped performance, the fabric-and-wood Weymann body gave complete silence without any sort of resonance, and almost negligible weight. Their only disadvantage, in the eyes of chauffeurs and some proud owners, was that they could not be polished and never gave the same satisfactory shine as half a dozen good coats of paint on steel or aluminium.

My 8-litre had beautifully comfortable seats (and few people today seem to recognize how important this is) and it had a great feeling of spaciousness.

It was about as quiet as a car can be and could do 110 m.p.h. on the open road without apparent effort. I modified it to my own requirements in several little ways. For instance, I used a proprietary American windscreen wiper which operated on a horizontal rod, one blade catching the other and carrying it in a companionable sort of manner to the side of the screen when parked. The 8-litre also had the very first Bosch trafficators, which never failed or jammed at any speed. Steady retrogression seems to be the guiding principle of some people who have made trafficators since then.

Also, for a time, the 8-litre was steam-cooled. Both Rolls-Royce and ourselves, with our huge engines, were having boiling troubles in hot climates and over mountain passes. This was hardly surprising with radiator blocks in the stage of development which applied at that time. It simply wasn't possible to fit one large enough to deal with the immense amount of heat given out by an engine of 6 or 7 litres under very demanding conditions.

As an experiment, then, we fitted a tank to the bottom of the radiator, and the water from this was pumped into the cylinders, when it overflowed and returned to the tank. In this way the cylinder was always full to a certain level, and when it steamed the steam went to the bottom above the water level and rose up the radiator's honeycomb, where it condensed and came down again as water.

I drove the 8-litre all over Europe and at full bore up every pass I knew without any trouble and never lost a drop of water. The advantage of this steam-cooling was that it was lighter and the car ran at a uniform temperature almost from the start.

We did have a little difficulty in getting a positive pump to drive the water into the cylinder block and the engine was rather noisier because the valve clearances had to be increased. But I think we would have got these difficulties ironed out, and we were approaching the production stage, when a new and much thinner and more satisfactory radiator block came on the market and got us out of this little bit of trouble. I believe the Americans were doing similar work at this time, as they were having trouble with their big engines, too. They called this modification 'evaporative' cooling. Cement-mixers and other machines that have to remain stationary for long periods operate their cooling on the same principle today.

The performance of that old 8-litre was extraordinary, even by modern standards, and in some respects it combined the merits of the 8-litre and 6½-litre Bentleys. With its lighter 6½ gearbox, axle and frame, the acceleration was tremendous, and the 8-litre engine made it only fractionally heavier. Just how spectacular the performance of that car was in 1930 can be judged by glancing at the Road Test of a standard 8-litre, included in the Appendices of this book. My own car was substantially lighter than this, of course, and the acceleration figures in particular much superior.

To digress a moment: we had a certain amount of trouble with the production 8-litre frame at first. The 6½ frame was not very rigid and was rather unsuitable for some of the heavy bodies that customers insisted upon, but the extra rigidity incorporated in the 8-litre frame produced complications which became evident when I began testing it. At that time there was almost no support between the dash and the dumbirons for cars with big heavy chassis. The result of this was that when the front axle vibrated up and down, the frame became excited in sympathy, and on the wrong frequency, with axle tramp resulting. I discovered this under hazardous circumstances. I was approaching a corner at just 80 m.p.h. when the tramp set in, and I got no results at all when I tried to steer round. I'm not sure to this day just how I got out of that one. This happened just before we were to deliver the first cars, so the long-term results of the episode looked as though they would be even more embarrassing. We were hard put to it to solve the problem entirely satisfactorily on the 8-litre, but we did so just in time by various modifications, including the mounting of rubber bushes to the bolts securing the body scuttle dash to the chassis dashboard. I tested the early cars individually myself before delivery at every possible speed and under every possible circumstance, to ensure this safety until I was satisfied that we had entirely cured this tramping nuisance.

Soon after this I witnessed the same trouble at Rolls-Royce with their first 3½ Rolls-Bentley. They later got round the difficulty ingeniously by modifying the front bumpers to carry a balance weight which travelled up and down and was timed to put the frame out of phase with the axle; a Wilmot-Breedon patent, I believe.

Because Rolls-Royce could not think of anything else to do with me after they bought me up in 1931 (my person was, in effect, part of the deal) they put me on to testing the early 3½ Rolls-Bentleys; and this car provided me with many months of pleasant motoring. It also gave me a few nasty moments, because I was supposed to do things with it that no private owner would contemplate attempting. I used to take this 3½ out from Derby and round a private circuit of my own. The main purpose of these runs was to test the brakes. It is necessary only to drive fast any quality car of the 1930s on the roads today to realize what tremendous advances have been made in brake development in the past quarter-century. Most modern drivers, with their disc-braked, 80-m.p.h. saloons, would be surprised by the brakes of a 1935 Rolls-Bentley by modern standards, although their servo system was about the best that could be had at the time, and it was efficient and light to operate. The one serious drawback was that it was prone to very sudden fade if the brakes were used continuously. With a top speed of around 90 m.p.h. the Rolls-Bentley was quite fast, too, and I learned on a recent trip up to Derby that I still hold the works record for the Red Gate–Derby run in a 3½-litre.

But it was a combination of axle tramp and brake fade that combined to finish my testing days once and for all. One day some time in 1936 I was putting the 3½ saloon through its paces, which meant treating the brakes unmercifully at corner after corner on my own special route to London. Unfortunately, someone had dropped a brick at the side of the road and on the apex of a rather nasty left-hand corner. I caught it with my nearside front wheel, and was at once subjected to the most appalling axle tramp. This meant I had no steering at all. So I tried to use the brakes, and found that I had none of these either, as they had faded quite away. With neither steering nor brakes, I calmly awaited my fate, curious to learn what I was going to hit. My victim was a Wolseley Hornet, approaching innocently and on the correct side of the road.

The little Wolseley was quite pulverized by the impact, which made an ear-splitting noise, hurled the owner harmlessly aside and threw me against the steering column. In a remarkably short space of time I was standing in the road beside the mass of rubble, finding my hand being shaken by the Wolseley owner, who was congratulating me on my merciful escape, and, instead of showing any hard feelings, helped me to replace a piece of the end of my nose that had been almost severed.

There was a police case after this episode, however, and for a time Rolls-Royce were anxious that there might be something more serious than the 'without due care and regard' summons that was eventually issued. I said, in perfect truth, that a tyre had burst, and was duly fined a modest £10. But I thought the magistrate gave me one or two curious glances during the proceedings, and on the way out of the court he took me aside and asked me in a confidential tone: 'Tell me, Mr Bentley, what did really happen? I know you use that road for testing your cars.' I gave him an enigmatic smile and passed on.

The Wolseley owner, by the way, got a new car from Rolls-Royce; there was never any argument about that. And I

never did such strenuous testing again; I found I had become
rather thoughtful.

Second to the D.F.P.s and my own cars, I suppose I have
done a greater mileage on the 3½ Rolls-Bentleys than any other
motor. It was, as I have said, very pleasurable motoring, too.
Soon after the first 3½s came on the market, I was asked to
take one across the Channel and do what I could to break it.
'Go anywhere you like,' I was told, 'for as long as you like.'
I left at once, taking my wife with me, and we had a very
pleasant seven weeks in France, Italy, Switzerland and Germany, going up and down all the passes I could find, and
doing long, fast runs between cities.

I found two main faults, which were later put right as a
result of this tour. One concerned the radiator shutters. On
one morning we did the Milan–Turin run of 120 miles at an
average of just 78 m.p.h., and we could have done much better
than this if I had not discovered that at sustained high speeds
the shutters were forced shut by the wind pressure, and the
water temperature consequently rose alarmingly, obliging me
to slow up momentarily until the needle dropped sufficiently.
The shutters were very effective on the passes, and I never had
a moment's concern about boiling. Coming down, however,
was different. I remember one evening descending the moun-
tains to Cannes, using third and accelerating briskly between
the hairpins, when the brakes faded until nothing was left.

I chanced upon my report on this trip the other day and
as an example of what used to occupy me in those days (and
also what cars used to suffer in my hands!) I think it might be
interesting to reproduce it in full:

3000 miles in France, Switzerland and Italy on 2–B–4

Route		*Miles*
1st day	Dieppe, Senz, Dijon, Pontarlier	390
2nd	Lausanne, Martigny, Brig, Gletch	210
3rd	Grimsel Pass, Rurka Pass, Oberalp Pass, Schyn Pass, Julier Pass, Ofen Pass, S. Maria	205

Route		Miles
4th	Stelvio Pass, Sondrio, Cadenabbia on Lake Como	160
5th	Como, Milan, Turin, Briancon, Galibier, Briancon	220
6th	Briancon, Cannes	265

Homeward Journey

1st day	Cannes, Saulier	420
2nd	Saulier, Dieppe	374

The following passes over 3000 feet were climbed:

	Feet
Stelvio	9050
Galibier	8400
Furka	8000
D'Isoard	7900
Julier	7500
Grimsel	7130
Ofen	7100
Oberalp	7620
Sestrieres	6660
Monte Genevre	6100
St Pierre	3800
Schyn	3400
La Faye	3300

The car contained two people and 240 lb. of luggage.

The first day's run across France was done in torrential rain, which practically never stopped. This severe test produced only one very small leak at the corner of the windscreen, the sunshine roof being perfectly watertight. Mud was, however, splashed over the engine and the front side of the dashboard. The windscreen wipers work rather slowly for this type of rain.

The car ran very well, but on cambered roads and on corners one felt the overhang weight of the luggage, making it more of an effort to control the car. On bad pavé the car was very objectionable —the wings, lamps, etc., being very unsteady and the weakness of the frame in front causing the bonnet and body to rattle; this is the worst feature of the car in my opinion.

The second day was also very wet, and after a short time the windscreen-wiper cable broke, putting both the windscreen wipers out of action. The roads had many corners, and working the windscreen wiper by hand became very tiresome. This is a most annoying thing to happen on a tour and is a big job to put right, as the cables are buried in the body.

The third day brought out the best of the car, and the way it climbed the various passes was a revelation, and I have never been in a car which made these roads appear so ordinary.

The weather was not hot—60° to 65°; the water temperature never rose above 78°.

It was a very enjoyable day's run; the cornering, the gearbox, acceleration and handiness of the car enabled one to appreciate the scenery without the effort usually associated with driving over these twisting and hilly roads.

The fourth day included the Stelvio Pass, with its forty hairpin corners on the way up, and there was never any doubt of getting round with quite a lot to spare. The air temperature was 65° and the highest water temperature was 80°. The acceleration between the corners was excellent in spite of the weight carried.

The back number plate was knocked off on one of the corners and went over the side of the road. This was not the first time this plate had been hit. This standard position is really too low. The front wings also get hit if you are taking corners which require full lock.

Fifth day. This day's run included the two Autostradas from Como, Milan and Turin, and 120 miles were covered at an average of 75 m.p.h. The Galibier was also climbed at the end of the day in an effortless way which I have never experienced before. Once again the water temperature was under 80°.

When driving fast between Como and Turin the water temperature varied between 78° and 95°, owing to the wind pressure closing the shutters, while the oil pressure dropped 7 lb. below the usual average pressure owing to the oil getting very hot.

Sixth day. During the day's run, while trying to keep a set average speed which meant going down one of the smaller passes using third gear for acceleration, and braking rather hard before the corners, after a very short time the brakes became very ineffective owing presumably to their getting very hot.

SUMMARY

Body details

1. Back number plate is too low.
2. Front wings have too little clearance when on full lock at outside edge.
3. Dust enters luggage compartment making the toolbox deep in dust. It also enters the fitted suitcases and makes one's clothes very dusty.
4. Window winder and door handles rattle owing to their getting very loose.
5. Wind roar round body is the most tiring feature of a long run and makes it almost impossible to talk without raising one's voice very considerably.

Chassis details

1. The weakness of the frame in front and the small and hard spring movement causes the car to be almost unbearable on bad pavé, and the wings, lamps, bonnet and body get rattled very badly, and is the most unpleasant feature of the car. It is also very bad when cornering on a road where there are bad potholes causing the front of the car to sidestep outwards.
2. Petrol consumption is very good—from 16 to 22 according to speed, etc. Oil consumption with these pistons (Aerolite) is very good, being over 2000 miles to the gallon. Very little water was put in the radiator.
3. The brakes squeak very badly—standard linings.
4. The petrol pumps supply petrol satisfactorily at 9000 feet and when temperature was 95° in the shade.
5. The car handles very much better when there is no weight in the luggage container.
6. P.100 headlamps do not make enough difference to glare when dimmed.

7. Esso or Azur petrol should be used. Some of the others are very bad and pink very badly, even when one-third retarded.
8. Although lamps were seldom used very little water had to be added to the accumulators.
9. No electrical troubles.

The 3½ Rolls-Bentley was almost as fast as the 4½-litre Bentley that we had first produced eight years earlier, and of course it was much lighter, and quieter with its six-cylinder engine. It also had the best gearbox—with synchromesh—that Rolls-Royce had ever produced. All that it seriously lacked was independent suspension at the front, and really fade-free brakes.

When I have mentioned this lack of independent front suspension, people have often retorted: 'If you were so keen on it why didn't you ever fit it into your own cars?' The answer was that at the time we designed the 6½- and 8-litre, independent front suspension was too elaborate, too expensive and not sufficiently developed, just as an effective four-wheel braking system was not ready for the first 3-litre cars. We should certainly have got round to it in time, and of course we included it in the V12 Lagonda specification in 1937.

I had nothing whatever, of course, to do with the designing of the 3½-litre Rolls-Bentley, but it was quite an interesting experience for me to be an observer and a witness to the growing-pains and development of the car, particularly as I had suffered so many of the same headaches with our own machines. I was, however, 'kept in the picture', as the saying goes, and I remember the conference that took place and the memoranda that were circulated on the subject of the engine for the new car—the 'Bensport' as it was called in the works For some months during 1932 experiments went on at Derby with Powerplus and Roots-type superchargers fitted on a small experimental engine and using aero-engine fuel.

This 25-h.p. engine, the J.1., with the induction on one side and exhaust on the other, had been designed to replace the 20/25-h.p. engine and provide the smaller Rolls-Royce with more power. This it did well enough, but at the expense of a noise level above R-R standards but well below contemporary sports-car standards. To use it in a new 'Bentley' seemed a sensible way of preventing it from going on the scrapheap.

As may be imagined, these supercharger tests were rigorous in the extreme and the higher power output achieved was treated with the gravest reserve. Derby were determined that the new car should have a sporting flavour, in the tradition of its predecessor. But no risks were going to be taken; there must be no shadow of chance that the huge and unique fund of goodwill possessed by the company might be jeopardized by an unreliable car, even one appearing under another name.

If I had been consulted, I think I could have saved Derby the expense and time involved in testing the 'Bensport' with a supercharged engine. Quite apart from any difficulties regarding royalties that would be payable for the use of Powerplus or Rootes-type superchargers, the necessity for owners to have to use special high-octane fuel every time they filled up had to be considered.

Even in 1932, when it was at the height of its fashionableness, the supercharger still had a distinct flavour of the race-track about it and this Rolls-Royce was determined to avoid at all costs. Quite apart from all these disadvantages, Rolls-Royce cars and the supercharger were temperamentally alien to one another. Very largely at Hives's persuasion, all ideas of using a supercharger, even a supercharger of their own manufacture, were finally dropped when gasket after gasket was blown during these trials, and the J.1. engine with atmospheric induction, which was all ready and awaiting a job, was used instead, with admirable results, in the chassis of the old experimental 18-h.p. Rolls-Royce.

Rationalization was not a word often used in the motor business in those days, while today, of course, no one pretends to differentiate between a Rolls-Royce and a Bentley, although,

A happy victory pile-up at Le Mans. Many of those present have since become distinguished figures in British engineering

Another jovial group, this time in the Isle of Man in 1922. From left to right: Sir Algernon Guinness, myself, Segrave, Kenelm Lee Guinness, Frank Clement

The four-cylinder Sizaire-Naudin I bought from Jarrott and Letts around 1910

My brother H.M.'s A.C. Sociable

1922 T.T. Bentley with offside wing being fitted at the last minute by Douglas Hawkes and his mechanic

as I believe the American advertisements put it, those who feel self-conscious about possessing a car with the square radiator can choose the alternative and save themselves a few dollars as well. But there was a certain sensitiveness at Derby about the use of standard Rolls components in a machine that did not bear the correct name, and I remember after a conference and test run at Brooklands with the first Bensport, now called the Bentley 3½-litre, 'The Silent Sports Car', that recommendations were made to design new types of milled nuts for the valve cover, new grips for brake and gear lever, a new petrol filler cap and floor mats with the letter 'B' engraved on them and numerous other minor modifications in order to distinguish the new car from its stable-mates.

At one period during my time with Rolls-Royce, between testing the cars used for demonstration by the London show-rooms and the main agents, I was asked to take to Brooklands other contemporary high-performance cars and submit reports on them in order that they could be judged against the Bentley. This gave me a welcome respite from driving Phantoms and the 3½s round the track and a chance to see what other people were up to.

The Lagonda, Alvis, V12 Hispano-Suiza (a surprising dis-appointment this) and several American machines were among those I tested, and I only wish that I could remember more precisely what I thought of these cars. But I do still have one or two of the reports, and the following one on the new Railton Terraplane, which I had heard could out-perform the 3½ Bentley while costing considerably less, may be interesting, and shows what I was looking for.

THE RAILTON TERRAPLANE

Weight: The car with a closed body weighs 25 cwt. (Bentley 31).
Engine size: The engine size is 4168 c.c. (Bentley 3669).
Gear ratio: The gear ratio is lower on top than in the Bentley closed car.

Acceleration: There is no magic, taking the above facts into consideration, in the Railton's having better top gear acceleration, at least up to 60 m.p.h.

Speed: Railton half-mile about 87. Lap speed about 83. Bentley half-mile about 93. Lap speed about 89.

General comparison: The car generally cannot in any way be compared with the Bentley. The V8 Ford compares very favourably, but I cannot see that you get very much for the extra £220.

Compression ratio: The compression ratio is so high that Ethyl fuel is essential, and even with this fuel the engine must be kept clean.

Brakes: The brakes are only fair and require heavy pressure.

Steering: The steering is fair.

Road-holding: The road-holding is fair, but with little feeling of security, too prone to tail-wag, inclined to roll.

Lock: Not as good as Bentley, in spite of short wheelbase, 9 ft. 8 in.

High speed: The car when running at high speed is fussy owing to the low top-gear ratio, making one want to change up, also there is the usual American engine roar at high speed.

Low speed: At low speed the engine smoothness is superior to that of the Bentley, the lower torque reaction making the low speed pick up much more free from vibration—with eight cylinders and a more flexible engine mounting one is less conscious of the torque impulses, which also make the idle running of the engine much smoother than the Bentley.

Body: The body is very crude, the finish is bad and the seats uncomfortable.

Gearbox: The gearbox is less silent than the Ford's. It is not easy to change—no synchromesh.

Generally: Finally, I could find little to justify it's being so much more expensive than the Ford.

One of the last cars I used before my post-war succession of Morris Minors, and the last car to influence in any way the design work for which I was responsible, was that likeable little machine, the front-wheel-drive Citroen. I ran one of these as a firm's car in 1939 and drove it for a good mileage before it went to Stan Ivermee, who, I believe, added several hundred thousand miles to the total before crashing it some four years ago.

By and large, the Citroen was a remarkably good car. Like most French machines, it always did what you expected it to do, and you never felt insecure driving it, no matter what the circumstances might be. Both the steering and the change mechanism were rather heavy, but one got used to this. There were times, too, when I longed for a fourth gear, particularly in hilly Devonshire country, I remember, when I was often caught between ratios and felt quite helpless.

Characteristic of its country of origin, you always knew that there were only four cylinders working for you under the bonnet, and I should have liked to try the Big 6, which must be a very pleasant handful of a motor car. The cornering and the road-holding on the Citroen were astonishingly good, as anyone knows who has driven one, and the manner in which it remained glued to the ground going round corners, no matter what the road surface might be, was most endearing. But best of all was the Citroen's gluttony for work. It seemed to relish being driven hard, and flat-out driving all day appeared to leave it refreshed and longing for more.

Sometimes that pleasant Citroen used to be subject to a minor vibration period when cornering fast on lock. This was only a slight nuisance, and was caused by the Carden shaft overrunning the engine at certain times and not at others, creating a non-constant velocity. I mention this only because the same thing, in a much more extreme form, cropped up at Lagondas when we were testing the prototype $2\frac{1}{2}$-litre Lagonda at Staines immediately after World War II.

For a long time we could not understand why, when travelling slowly in top with practically no throttle, the engine appeared to miss. This was all the more curious because when carrying only one passenger under identical circumstances we had no trouble with the engine at all.

I don't know how long we all wasted on this annoying snag before the answer suddenly occurred to us. Of course, we at last reasoned, with the extra weight at the rear, the angle was altered between the bevel-box and the wheels and we might be subjecting the Carden shaft to a non-constant velocity. At last our reasoning was right, the vibration occasioned giving an almost identical impression to that caused by a missing engine.

At that time I believe there was only one foreign firm making constant velocity joints, and as it was quite impossible to get supplies, we 'faked-up' this vibration period, quite successfully, too. I don't know whether Alec Issigonis and his team met this same trouble with the prototype Mini-Minor, but I was interested to see, when the specification of this car was published, that the design included a constant velocity joint. It would be interesting to know if any other design teams have met the same trouble, and have been as mystified as we were with the Lagonda.

I think now that I ought really to have driven more cheap 'bread-and-butter' cars during my active years as a designer, and indeed it was not even my choice that I drove one model almost daily for several years. It came about in this way.

After I had been 'bought' by Rolls-Royce and told to hand over to Jack Barclay my own 8-litre car, I found myself in the unusual position of being without personal transport. This was the first time since about 1910, when cars were still comparatively rare anyway, that I had not had one. It was a curious feeling. I had to use buses and Tubes, and I didn't like this much, so I took to walking instead, which was probably better for me, but rather slow. At that time I could barely have afforded the down payment on the cheapest on the market, and, though I hope I didn't tell anyone my dilemma, Billy Rootes must have divined the reason behind my curious and uncharacteristic new habit of tramping from point to point about London.

Billy Rootes (now Lord Rootes, of course) had been an active and successful agent for Bentleys, and I knew him quite well by then; well enough, anyway, for him to be able to ask me, without so much as a blush, whether I wouldn't mind doing him a favour. 'I'd be very grateful if you'd try this car,' he told me on the telephone one day. 'I want your honest opinion on it.'

The car in question was one of the new Hillman Minxes, and for that particular week-end, and for almost every week-end for months afterwards, a Minx or one of their larger cars used to be made available to me. This was not only a great convenience, but I could quite honestly tell him that I thought the Minx was a very nice little car.

I have never forgotten this kindly and thoughtful gesture of Rootes at a time when things were not going so well for me. He has not only deserved all the success he has had, but has reached his present distinguished position by honesty and integrity as well as kindness. I should doubt if he has any enemies.

Some months later I was able to purchase a Minx for myself, on the specially favourable terms Rootes offered me, and from then until the beginning of the war I was never without one, although they were really my wife's cars.

I must say, though, that I was rather doubtful about going to the South of France in a Hillman Minx after always doing the journey previously in somewhat swifter and more robust machines. However, I was lucky to have a car at all, and set out with my wife, a considerable weight of luggage and some nervousness. But I was soon surprised at how game and robust the Minx was, and how effortlessly one could drive 350 miles in a day in it. It was hardly a grand tourer, but the only trouble we had was with tyres, suffering five punctures by the time we reached Le Mans, where I purchased some more suitable ones.

A Standard 8 scarcely seemed a suitable machine for the long trek to the sun, either; but, like the Minx, it surprised me by its willingness and ability to slog along all day at a reasonable average. I had one of these for a short time after the war, and did many thousands of miles in it. The road-holding was hardly brilliant, and of course it was never intended to suffer the liberties I took with it on one hurried return from the South of France, but it was quite a good little car.

The only car I drive regularly now is the nice little Morris Minor, of which more later.

2

Motor Bicycles and Brooklands

T HE four-wheeled vehicle with its internal combustion engine that we call the motor car has given me much pleasure, as well as pain and disappointment. But I am not sure now whether I do not resent the manner in which it has intruded, filling far too much of my life and leaving me with insufficient time to explore so many other fields in which I am interested, like meteorology and wireless telegraphy.

Perhaps I regret now a little that I made the motor industry my profession, if only because for so long the machines filled my life to the exclusion of almost everything else. I sometimes wonder if I should not have stuck to those fine, powerful and friendly things—locomotives.

The locomotive started it all for me, and if the railways had provided me with a living to the standards I considered necessary, I should probably have stuck with them. But it was a sad parting, and I always missed them through the years of aero-engine and car designing. It was, in fact, while I was working on locomotives at Doncaster that I became a motor-bicycling enthusiast; and I certainly got more pure *fun* out of the motor bicycle than I ever got from any of my cars, although I willingly accept that sport on two wheels is essentially for the young, and for me it was only a sport, with no commercial purpose behind it.

[37]

I look back now with great affection on those days of motor-bicycle competition in Edwardian times, before I was afflicted by the car 'bug'. All the events run by the Auto Cycle Union and Motor Cycling Club possessed an excellent spirit of friendly, co-operative, uncommercialized competitiveness. I do not remember a single hill-climb, sprint, trial or Brooklands race in which this spirit was not present. It was not unusual to see competitors helping one another by the roadside, or making last-moment adjustments to one another's machines just before a race.

I discovered very sharply just how tough competition work was when, without any previous experience, I entered my 3-h.p. Quadrant for the London–Edinburgh Trial. This Quadrant, with its surface carburettor, was rather like an unreliable and uncomfortable present-day motorized bicycle to drive. Any healthy young man today would gladly take his motorized bicycle from London to Edinburgh; that would be no great achievement, if quite hard work pedalling up some of the steeper hills. But we had to do this journey to a tight schedule on roads that in places seemed not to have been touched since they broke up after the Roman occupation. It took a day and night to accomplish, and the only food was at the control points; but I was always too late at these to have time to eat and did the trip on apples and chocolate as I went along. To my astonishment, I got a gold medal, too!

I did a lot of these endurance trials after this, enjoying both the spirit behind them and the sense of independent competitiveness out on the open road that they inspired. I did them mostly on Rexs and Indians; London to Exeter, London to Land's End and back several times, London to Plymouth and back; and each was a really testing challenge to your endurance and your mechanical aptitude, for, of course, breakdowns were frequent.

Some of the hill-climbs, too, were really devastating, and the competition very close, with a fifth of a second often separating the three or four fastest times. Events I remember particularly were those run at Kop Hill near Great Missenden in Buckinghamshire and at Sharpenhoe near Luton, and of course those great runs up Snaefell in the Isle of Man after the Tourist Trophy races. As these became more popular their importance became recognized by the factories, and works teams began to appear.

Naturally these works teams soon dominated the hill-climbs, and I had great sport as an independent trying to beat them. With experience I began to get the hang of tuning my 5-h.p. Indian, lightening the pistons and putting up the compression and generally fiddling, until I began to put up faster times than the works riders, which gave me more pleasure than anything. In fairness I should add that I got every sort of help from the factory, who were quite happy so long as an Indian won!

Motor-bicycle racing at Brooklands was a tame business after the T.T. and hill-climbs. Brooklands races were usually short sprints or one-hour events, with the results depending less on the riders than the machines. There was not much finesse involved in racing on Brooklands, except perhaps in avoiding the worst bits of surface. I have never believed that Edge's run on the Napier soon after it was opened was responsible for the poor surface from which Brooklands suffered. This was always worse towards the top of the bankings, and I don't think that the builders ever succeeded in satisfactorily blending this top section. Even in the earliest days they always seemed to be mending parts of the tracks, and this was not always as well done as it could have been, with the consequence that it never got over this roughness.

We missed the worst bumps on the bankings on our motor bicycles, which rarely lapped at much over 70 m.p.h., but I do remember the severe roughness coming off the Members' Banking on to the Railway Straight. On the Straight itself one just went to sleep, it was so boring.

I began to learn much more about the subtleties of Brooklands when I began to race and carry out record attempts there in cars. The really difficult part, which required much practice to perfect, was the fast bend at the Fork. On a bike one hardly noticed this, but when lapping in the nineties in the D.F.P., for example, it took some time to get the hang of holding down low enough from the Byfleet Banking at the Fork in order to take full advantage of the very steep Members' Banking that followed. It was always a temptation to stay too far to the right at the Fork, and so be badly placed for the Banking that followed.

I did more record-breaking than racing at Brooklands before World War I, but found them both fun. Quite a lot was in fact at stake for us as D.F.P. concessionaries, and the ding-dong battle I had with Tuck and his Humber was most exciting, until I at last succeeded in the special single-seat aluminium-bodied 12/40 D.F.P. to take the Class B records out of his reach.

One of the things I learnt particularly when I was after the longer records was discretion. I dare say Tuck discovered this, too, though we never discussed the matter; but I found it very worth while to ease up briefly once on every lap in order to let the engine suck up oil. I found it made all the difference to the reliability factor, and the loss in time was negligible.

In the two years before the outbreak of World War I, sport and business combined very happily for me. With the sort of car we were selling at that time (mainly the quite sporty 12/15 and 12/40 D.F.P.s imported from France), it really was important to demonstrate its prowess at competition events. Even more than today, the young bloods of that period who were drawn to motors made their choice of machine from the car that performed well in sprints and hill-climbs.

Brooklands events did not count for so much because the cars that raced there were mostly 'specials' or unrecognizably modified standard cars. On the other hand it did matter greatly to, say, the Humber, Star, Argyll or Arrol-Johnston factories whether their machines performed creditably at hill-climbs, sprint events on sand, or took or lost Class Records at

Brooklands. From our own experience at Bentley and Bentley as concessionares for the D.F.P. we knew that a well-publicized 'fastest time' at a hill-climb event at the week-end would bring customers in to the showrooms during the following week.

With so much at stake, some of these more important sprints and hill-climbs became very competitive, and, strictly within the regulations of course, no holds were barred. Most of the sprint events, except those at the Brooklands track, took place on sand at places like Southport and Saltburn. One driver in particular had a special knack for persuading other competitors into the softer, damper sand, which had been carefully re-connoitred before. Another trick he had, which required some practice, was to swing the tail round hard alongside a fellow competitor and spray him with sand like an excited dog scratching for a bone. This could be highly painful, as well as distracting, for the offended party, as I found to my cost on more than one occasion. On the whole I did not get much fun out of racing on sand.

I got much more fun out of the hill-climbs. There was a very adventurous atmosphere about them, as if we were all pioneers in something that would one day become important and, inevitably, lose its personal appeal. We would all arrive, driving the cars we had entered, at the appointed place in the morning and gather at the nearest railway station. There the machines would be weighed, as most of the events were run on a weight and engine capacity formula basis. The weighing-in on the doubtfully accurate machine borrowed from the railway company would be followed with the closest interest by all the competitors, usually accompanied by critical remarks on the amount of chassis-drilling carried out by some enthusiast.

I'm afraid sharp practice was occasionally resorted to, too. There was, for example, the driver who had an extraordinary run of successes and was almost unbeatable in his class in the formula events until it was discovered that his car had a built-in concealed water tank, which was filled before the weighing-in and surreptitiously emptied on the way to the starting line.

Aston Clinton in Hertfordshire was one of the most important annual hill-climb events, and it was here that we had one of our earliest and most useful successes by making fastest time with the D.F.P. Now that I am seventy-two, and drive a Morris Minor only with discretion, I can look back with indulgent nostalgia to these memorable seconds when I used to sit at the wheel, with the clutch out and right foot poised on the accelerator, awaiting the fall of the starter's flag, and then the storming rush up the winding hill ahead. Those hill-climbs were good fun.

3

The Life Preservers

Everyone who drives, or walks, on the roads of Britain today is conscious of the injustices and irritations that exist, partly by reason of the tremendous but readily anticipated increase in traffic, and partly because of hopelessly muddled and mean Government policy extending back at least thirty years. We all know about the chaotic conditions and we all know that the real root of the trouble has been the continuing refusal of the Government—because of ineptitude and the fact that there are no votes and no political advantages to be gained —to spend money. It is as simple as that.

We can all cite personal examples of idiocy among our local highway authorities. Around the part of Surrey in which I live large double-decker buses run on a main road which is so narrow that they cannot drive without encroaching over the centre white line on to the other half of the road. When they meet one has to stop and draw in hard against the bank. Many of the stops are placed on the brows of hills or on blind corners. The country bus has been with us for half a century, and yet only now and very slowly are parking bays being provided for them at stops. For several miles there is no pavement or footpath for pedestrians, and at night it is really safe to drive only very slowly for fear of meeting, say, a woman pushing a pram home from the shops—and there are many of them.

This is typical, as are the signs, some scarcely legible from old age, which warn of 'Very Dangerous Corner' and 'Dangerous When Wet'. I know that some of these have been up for forty years—and still the corners are dangerous and still the road surface is dangerous when wet! I wonder how many more will die or be maimed before anything is done.

This state of affairs exists all over the country, and when a pedestrian is killed or a cyclist knocked down by a driver edging out from behind a stationary bus at night, it is not the driver against whom criminal proceedings should be taken. It is the local highway authority who should be in the dock, and who should go to prison for manslaughter. Yes, I feel as strongly as that about it! Many of the fatal situations that occur on the roads today are the result of criminal folly by local civil servants and the Ministry of Transport, and a test case against one of them for causing a fatal accident would cause a satisfactory flutter in many a County Council highways department.

The discomfort and waste caused by inadequate roads would, though, be more tolerable if there were less cant and hypocrisy and plain stupidity in attempting to control the motorist. I think this is caused in part because as a nation we have never grown up as far as the motor car is concerned. In contrast to America and France, Germany and Italy, authority is still reluctant to accept the very existence of the motor vehicle, which is regarded, in our highly class-ridden society, as something faintly naughty and self-indulgent, or the plaything of a rich minority. Every motorist who steps into his car drives away with the feeling, to a lesser or greater degree according to his nature, that he is, if not a marked man, at least already doing something very close to breaking the law. And, of course, so muddled and complex is our legislation relating to the motorist that he probably *has* broken the Highway Code if not the law in one way or another within the first ten miles.

If it is not the law nor the Highway Code that the motorist has offended he will certainly have acted against the strictures of some self-appointed authority. 'A good driver,' some ass announces, 'always holds the steering wheel at the ten-to-three position.' Or it may be twenty to four, half past six or something equally idiotic. But this, like many other facets of driving, is something that must depend on the individual driver and the car. One driver may find his arm aches or fouls a window winder in this position. Another has a car with a steering column that is fixed as to rake and length which makes it dangerously inconvenient to hold the wheel at twenty to four.

'You must always drive with the arms outstretched,' pontificates another authority, 'like Stirling Moss. He should know.' What is good for Stirling Moss at the wheel of a Grand Prix car lapping Rheims at 125 m.p.h. may not be either safe or convenient for an elderly woman running in to the village to do the family shopping—probably in a car with a seat that will slide back only six inches from the steering wheel anyway. But our elderly woman will be worried when she finds that she is not apparently driving correctly; and she has enough worries on her mind avoiding the cyclists on the way to the village.

The standard driving test demands that hand signals should always be given when slowing up, stopping and when turning right or left. Here is more evidence of the suicidally archaic attitude of authority. It is as if the Ministry of Transport were unaware of the fact that the brake light and electric signal had ever been invented. I believe that, except in unusual circumstances, when the greater range of expression or emphasis a hand signal offers is useful, all signalling should be done by the excellent mechanical contrivances that clever people have taken the trouble to invent.

It is just when you are turning or slowing down in traffic that both hands should be on the wheel instead of groping for a window winder and then projecting an arm into the airstream. If they were able to do so I do believe that the Government would pass legislation making it obligatory for jet-liner pilots to signal by hand their intention to land! But, seriously, is there any more frightening sight than a learner driver going through a roundabout at dusk in rush-hour traffic fighting to keep control of the steering wheel with the left hand (and changing gear with it, too, of course) while waving an arm in frantic gestures to duplicate what winkers and brake lights have already clearly told those behind?

Then I believe some body that tests drivers and issues them with badges if they meet their stringent demands fail (or passes, I forget which) drivers who keep their hands at the same place on the wheel when turning corners. This seems very odd to me. Do their testers, I wonder, take regard of the make of the car that the victim is driving? Do they check up first to see whether it is an A.C., with steering that requires two turns from lock to lock, or a Humber with a wheel that has to be turned more than twice as many times?

I do not intend to be facetious; I am only trying to point out that driving is essentially a *personal* business, and the law, and near-law, seeks all the time to restrict the motorist in so many ways that in another generation or two he will either have to do a year's legal training before taking to the road or retire quietly to Broadmoor. Having filled the road verges and pavements with so many notices instructing and informing drivers where to go and what to do that pedestrians are hard put to it to find somewhere to walk, authority is now busily adding to the bewildering total by painting more on the roads themselves.

Actually I don't think this is a bad thing in itself, and if we had restricted all road signs to the roads from the beginning we should be the better, and saner, for it. Double white lines, for instance, are fundamentally sensible, but I think the dotted line confuses things and is difficult to spot if you are close to another car. Personally I should be happier with a yellow line which must not be crossed by either up or down traffic.

The ingenious French, I believe, invented double white lines, and we did well to imitate them, even if it did take us

1914 Tourist Trophy D.F.P., showing the high standard of hand metal-beating we could expect in those days

On the weighbridge at Douglas

Prototype six-cylinder Bentley with camouflaged radiator shell
at Le Mans

Phantom II Continental Rolls-Royce which I tested extensively
in the Alps

ten years. But they are often so misapplied in Britain that I can't help feeling that they are at present taking more lives than they are saving.

I think the main trouble is that they are laid out by local officials, some of whom have the most meagre knowledge of what is a safe and what is a dangerous place to pass, and how long it takes to do so. I shudder to think what the result would be if drivers pulled out to pass at some of the places round my part of the world where they are given the 'all clear'. Fortunately, most drivers are more intelligent than public authorities give them credit for. If they weren't they would wait all day at white lines beside Halt Major Road Ahead signs at intersections which prohibit the view in both directions down the main road.

Everybody obviously wants everything that can be done within the realms of reason to keep as low as possible the casualty rate on the roads. But this question of road deaths always seems to be seen out of true focus. What is much more remarkable, although the fact is hardly worth newspaper headlines, is the vast number of lives that motorists save year after year.

At the risk of being thought callous, I would say that the astonishingly low road-death rates in this country are one of the real miracles of the age. Here we are sending almost all our goods traffic (and even coal now!) on a road system that has scarcely improved since Roman times when the freight trains run empty and lose millions a year; here we are insisting quite sensibly on our right to travel in our millions fifty or a hundred miles for a few hours by the sea, or travelling for week-ends distances that it would have taken our grandparents a week to accomplish; here we are, quite sensibly, insisting on motoring in comfort, with wireless and heater, to our offices morning and evening rather than in an overcrowded railway carriage; here we are spending perhaps five or even fifty per cent of our waking lives in vehicles often within a few feet of other vehicles passing in the opposite direction at a closing speed of 90 m.p.h.; here we are with all the conveniences and comforts and the broadening of minds that the motor car provides—and we expect to do it all without paying any price for it!

That the price is so low is incredible. Why, more people were killed by *falls* in 1958 than on the roads. That only one in ten thousand of us dies every year under the circumstances I find almost beyond belief. And yet this evader supreme, this brilliant life-saver, this genius in the art of self-survival, is hounded and bullied, reprimanded like a prep-school boy, taken to court, and bled white by an exchequer that has either evil intentions or a perverted sense of humour.

As we shall quite clearly never get an adequate road system in this country that will separate completely pedestrians, drivers of two-wheel vehicles and other traffic, I do think it is time that some of the burden of responsibility should now be placed on another road-user. I refer of course to the sort of pedestrian (and we are all pedestrians at some time) who makes it a point of defiance never to use a zebra crossing even if he has to go out of the way not to do so; the mother who pushes a pram far out into the traffic stream against the lights; and all those pedestrians who flirt with death either absentmindedly or deliberately irresponsibly—especially on Saturday nights outside the pubs.

No one in their right minds can be against the principle of road legislation that will make driving safer and more pleasant. It is foolish legislation that makes us angry and frustrated. There is talk at present of some diabolical instrument called, I believe, a breathylizer, to test whether a driver has had so much to drink that he is incapable of driving a car. I suppose it registers something on a dial. Does it also take into account, I wonder, the age and general state of health of its victim? His susceptibility to alcohol? Whether he has been to a noisy party and has to drive home in the dark on icy roads a car that is tricky to handle? Or whether he is a doctor, home for a quick sherry after a hard day's work and called out to an emergency case? This sort of thing just doesn't make sense to me. Next it will be a reaction-tester—regardless of the fact that a good driver should *never* be surprised, *never* have suddenly to do anything.

If the time and money spent on idiotic and unnecessary legislation were spent, as an interim measure, on simplifying and making road signs uniform, widening roundabouts, cutting blind corners instead of warning of them, and making surfaces safe when wet instead of warning that they are dangerous when wet; if a hundred-and-one obvious correctives that we can all think of could be carried out with the speed that Beaverbrook produced fighters for us in the Battle of Britain, then we should be on the way to sanity. And the members of the safety society who litter the road verges with distracting signs everywhere would have even less cause for concern at the casualty figures.

If the numbers of those killed driving motor bicycles and scooters are subtracted from the total death figures on the roads the result is even more startling. And on the subject of motor bicycles in particular I do think there is room here for *sound* legislation. Until very recently the law permitted a boy of sixteen to buy and drive a 500-c.c. motor bicycle without any previous experience, even on a motorized bicycle.[1] This does seem dangerous to me. Some of these bigger motor cycles have the acceleration of a Grand Prix car and a top speed of well over a hundred miles an hour.

When I was still much too young I had a huge Indian motor cycle which I often drove at night at over 80 m.p.h. and did things with it which I remember only with horror—and amazement that I am still alive. I loved showing off on it, just as it is quite natural and healthy for any young man to show off and experience that heady, exciting sensation of speed that only a fast motor bicycle can produce. But I really don't think that it would be a greater infringement on the liberty of the individual to restrict the sale of these very fast machines to older and more experienced riders than it is, say, to prohibit

---

[1] From July 1st, 1961, under the Hughes Hallett Act, a limit of 250 c.c. was imposed on learner motor-cyclists.

the sale of dangerous drugs or carry out any other sensible safety precautions. It seems unfair to make it so easy for young people to kill themselves, and very often their innocent pillion passengers.

I know other people are concerned about these big-engined motor cycles, and I mention them at the risk of crippling my argument that it is only the wrong speed at the wrong moment that is a major danger on the roads. I feel this very strongly. There are many arguments put forward in support of this, but the one I always feel is most telling is that most people drive at the speed at which they consider themselves safe and comfortable. That this has risen slightly, but not by nearly so much as has the cruising speed of the average production car, is not a danger in itself because suspension, brakes and steering have more than kept pace with this increase.

The minority always have done and always will drive at a speed above their capacity to anticipate danger, and these people will continue to use the roads while the motor car remains as a form of transport. If every car was fitted with a governor limiting its speed to, say, 40 m.p.h. these people would remain as strong a danger element, using their maximum permitted speed rashly in dense traffic where most of the casualties occur, anyway. It is no coincidence that the safest stretch of road in Britain is also the fastest. Nowhere in Britain do average motorists drive so rapidly as on our first motorway, and nowhere is it safer for him to do so.

In spite of the posters that catch our eyes (usually when they should be on the road) informing us that speed kills, it is not speed but bad roads and *bad speeds*, whether too fast or too slow for the conditions, that kill. Bad roads mean not just inadequate roads for the volume of traffic, but roads subjected to stupid legislation and stupid control by local authorities. We have these in abundance in Britain—and their unsung heroes are the men and women who drive on them.

4

The Bentley That Never Will Be . . .

I DON'T believe it likely that I shall ever be responsible for the design of another motor car, nor do I flatter myself that this is any great tragedy. Conditions have changed tremendously, even to the extent that now almost no single individual is responsible for the design of a motor car in the meaning of the function in my day. New methods of production, new materials, new demands, have all arrived since I last sat down to think up a new motor car. I am unfamiliar with so many modern developments that I am best out of it all today. Nor do I mind very much; the last words of this book will show you why.

Nevertheless, I still toy with ideas when I am not sleeping very well, although I am really only seriously interested now in the kind of car I want to own myself—and pay the upkeep. Sometimes somebody is kind enough to ask me: 'What sort of motor car would you produce today if you were starting from scratch?' I don't mind in the least when people ask me this question—why should I?—but I do have to ask the questioner to elaborate. What sort of motor car for what sort of public? How much money is there available? What production facilities do I have? Above all, how much time do I have?

To start with, I don't think I would agree to tackle a large luxury car again. I am no longer interested in the large car and would not run one if it were given to me and the running costs paid for, and today the hand-built luxury car is hardly a serious proposition; World War II, the Welfare State and the increase in labour costs have seen to that. While certain people still insist on flaunting their wealth and success to the world, there will continue to be a demand for the luxury car. But today, when improved methods of production have raised the standard of the mass-produced car so high, the margin of greater merit of the luxury car over the larger higher-priced car (say a 3-litre Rover or a Vanden Plas Austin A99) is so minute that it is foolish to buy one except to show the firm's flag or as a personal status symbol.

Why spend six or seven thousand pounds on a luxury car when for less than a quarter of this price you can buy vice-free handling, perfect comfort, near-silence, a top speed of well over 100 m.p.h., with acceleration to match, and reliability? By all the laws of reason anyone today who spends more than £2000 of his own money on a motor car ought to have his head examined! There is, in any case, with the honourable exception of the Rolls-Royce and Bentley, no such thing as a hand-built luxury car today; the best that you can do for yourself is a car made largely of standard mass-produced components but more carefully assembled and tested and finished.

So let us leave out of the reckoning this vehicle. Instead, I think I would most like to tackle a small car. Not an austerity motor, nor a real baby. Just a simple down-to-earth car, to carry four in comfort, with an engine of about one litre, designed to be built in real numbers; for quantity is, in the long term, the most important factor in car manufacturing.

First of all I would not take the job on if I had to do it in a hurry, not only because I am getting on in years but because I should like time for development work. For the same reason I think I would eschew air-cooling. There is a tremendous field for development work in air-cooled engines as most people know and as I discovered at first hand when I produced a flat-four air-cooled for a special purpose three or four years ago. (It is still running quite happily in a Morris Minor somewhere.)

But air-cooling would take too long to perfect for my

purpose. There are, besides, two main disadvantages to the air-cooled engine in a small car. One is the question of noise-level. Noise to my mind is one of the major bugbears and miseries of motoring and must be reduced to the lowest possible level. At present an air-cooled engine is always noisier than a water-cooled engine of similar size. Resonance always seems to come through somehow, especially from the head. The only answer so far is to shut the engine up, to box it right away where it can't be heard, and no one has yet learnt how to do that successfully.

The second disadvantage is a purely negative one, and that is that the merits of air-cooling are little revealed in this temperate climate. In parts of the North American continent, and in certain European countries, air-cooling is, of course, highly advantageous, and this accounts in part for the tremendous success of the Volkswagen. But I can see little point in it for England.

My engine would, then, be water-cooled, and also orthodox in most of its features: four-in-line cylinders, pushrod overhead valves, with big bores to allow room in the head for reasonable-sized valves, probably over-square in dimensions, and with a quite high compression ratio.

I have no fear at all of a high compression ratio nowadays, although I think we are approaching the useful limit. This limit is not imposed by the petroleum chemists. I was talking recently to someone high up in the Standard Oil Company of America, and he claimed that all the oil companies were far ahead of the car manufacturers in octane values. 'We can always make better petrol for them,' he said.

But, as I explained to this man—though I have no doubt that he knew already—it is very difficult physically to get the combustion space small enough to give the higher compressions permitted by these advanced fuels without other disadvantages. For instance, the best head—the classic hemispherical—can't be used without a deformed piston. And if you use a comic head, you have to have valves to match which do not achieve adequate cooling. The bigger the engine, the easier this problem is to solve, as it was in America many years ago. But for an engine of around 1000 c.c. a compression ratio of about nine to one is the limit for normal purposes.

We would not aim at an unreasonably high power output from this engine. A great deal of nonsense is talked these days about engine power. That the average general public demands above all else a powerful engine is another one of the delusions the motor manufacturers are inclined to create for themselves— like these sudden, unpredictable and quite unwarranted enthusiasms they instil in their customers for four cylinders rather than six, or six cylinders in preference to four.

We have all seen these cycles repeated time and again. In the mid 'thirties no self-respecting manufacturer would dare to leave the six-cylinder car out of his catalogue, even if its capacity were barely one litre. A few years ago the Americans informed their car-buying public that 300 b.h.p. was the absolute minimum that they must accept—and of course a body length of at least seventeen feet. Now, of course, every self-respecting United States citizen buys a compact with an especially economical engine.

Even in this country ninety per cent of the drivers do not utilize the full output of their engines, and the 'fast' driver is always astonished, when perhaps running in a new car at a maximum of 45 m.p.h., how rarely he is passed. A high maximum speed is not something that I should aim at. I have always been much more interested in the speed to which the average driver settles down when he is on a clear road, with no obstructions, as on a motorway. This is the comfortable cruising speed of the car, which is vastly more important than the maximum and could well be included as a figure, which would not be difficult to assess, in road tests conducted by the motoring press. This comfortable cruising speed is also much more important than perhaps most of us realize and I wish more regard were paid to it. Of course, the nearer this speed is to the car's maximum, the more efficient the car is. A high top gear is, therefore, essential, even in this country. Simply by raising the back-axle ratio of my own Morris Minor 1000, which is already much higher geared than its predecessor, I have transformed its feel and much increased its comfortable cruising speed.

I am not going to venture into the complex and highly emotional subject of body styling, but before leaving the entertaining if hardly realistic subject of our new small car I should like to make a passing reference to driver and passenger comfort.

Mattress manufacturers sensibly sell their products on the assumption that their customers will live for a third of their lives on them, and energetic salesmen in bedding shops press this point home as they pummel the springs before their customers.

Although many purchasers of cars spend almost as long in them as they do in their beds, I have not yet seen a motor salesman follow this sales line as he takes the seat beside the customer for a demonstration run. Nor is this surprising. Nothing has deteriorated so deplorably in the past ten years as the seats in the cheaper motor car. I am sure the reason, as always, is one of cost and that it is not deliberate policy to make a drive of more than an hour or two a nightmare of discomfort.

One British manufacturer has already made a step in the right direction, and I should certainly insist that our driving seat is correctly shaped to hold the motorist's poor suffering torso and made adjustable for rake as well as fore-and-aft movement.

Another important comfort and safety factor is the position of the steering wheel, and I should have the rake and length of column adjustable. I do not believe that these refinements could cost in all more than ten pounds, even by today's inflated prices.

An absolute essential is wet cylinder liners. There is but one revolutionary feature in our 'new' small car, and this is that, as far as costs, ingenuity, planning and production methods permit, it is going to be as maintenance-free and trouble-free as we can devise it.

It seems quite incredible to me, and I do not believe that it is excusable, that in this day and age motor cars are still being produced that require greasing as frequently as every thousand miles. This is a mileage that many commercial travellers, and others, too, travel in little more than a week. Imagine being a sales representative travelling Western England and having not only to calculate where your next thousand miles will take you, but arranging in advance to have your car serviced at a garage which, if it is as busy as most, demands at least a week's notice! Such frequent maintenance is just as inconvenient for holiday-makers, country housewives who do a lot of motoring and for all those who use their cars to take them to work. Nor is it frivolous to point out that many farmers in the Commonwealth are so distant from a town that they are forced either to do the job themselves or, if they follow the manufacturers' instructions, use their car only to drive to and from the nearest service station!

I sometimes find myself wondering, only to put the thought aside as uncharitable, whether some manufacturers do not insist on this frequent maintenance to please their dealers, for whom it is a substantial form of income. That the problem can be solved has been shown by one manufacturer who has recently produced a cheap small car that doesn't need a grease gun for the first ten thousand miles. Why can't everyone do that? We got round the problem in the $2\frac{1}{2}$-litre Lagonda by lubricating by oil and fitting a can of it under the bonnet, where it could feed oil to the wishbone front suspension and swivel pins by gravity. It also did this automatically by means of a little ball valve, which, under vibration due to road irregularities when the car was moving, leapt off its seating and allowed oil to pass, but remained seated when the car was stationary. It worked quite well, too. Of course, it was costly then, and would be now—until such a system was put into quantity production, when, like such luxuries of old as four-wheel brakes, it could be produced economically.

I'm afraid I also refuse to believe that the cheap car cannot be made a great deal more trouble-free than it is now. A certain German firm has already shown that it is possible, but deplorably few other manufacturers have made much progress since the war. This is something I just cannot understand. It is a great annoyance to have to take back to the dealer who sold it to you a new car perhaps half a dozen times for trifling complaints to be rectified. As all manufacturers guarantee their cars for six or twelve months and have to pay for this fault-correcting, the expense must be reflected either in reduced profits or in a higher purchasing price; and it is not hard to guess which!

I have specified wet cylinder liners in my mythical small car, and obviously there is nothing very startling in this. I believe several million small and absurdly cheap French cars have been made since the war with wet liners and I can think of no reason why they should not be incorporated in equivalent British engines. Instead, the British motoring public seems to have become reconciled to the expense of a re-bore at perhaps thirty or forty thousand miles. I really don't see why it should be necessary, having spent six or seven hundred pounds on a new car, that perhaps another thirty pounds should be paid after another two years or so on a re-bore.

I believe the big manufacturers have for years been making the great mistake of under-estimating the damage caused by nuisance troubles to the goodwill they spend so much money and time in building up for their firm. Often you hear people complaining that they have had to take their new car back to the dealer time and again for some trifling trouble, traceable to careless assembly or workmanship. We have all known people who have had to take a certain make of car back three or even four times for a particularly notorious gearbox to be replaced. Why, over the years, has not this mammoth organization, making profits in tens of millions annually, done something about this congenital malady in its gearboxes? It seems to me that a few thousands spent on research might lead to a financial saving in the long run; and I can't help feeling that it would create better goodwill, and increased sales.

At some time in the future the manufacturers will have to face up to the fact that their customers will expect and demand a reliable, trouble-free product. I think the reason for this unreal state of affairs is that, except for brief periods of crisis, the manufacturers have for too long been living in an unreal period in which everything has gone their way and they have not had to try. For some fifteen years development has been limited almost entirely to re-clothing and re-vamping existing and long-obsolete designs. But there are signs now (in the autumn of 1960) that these manufacturers are having to face what the late John Foster Dulles called an agonizing reappraisal.

I should like to add just one more point to this question of reliability and maintenance, and here I am invading a new field of controversy on which I know very little. But isn't it possible that the people responsible for advertising are not making a mistake in failing to emphasize, when it applies, the reliability and the ease and simplicity of maintenance of motor cars?

I believe that an advertisement campaign loudly proclaiming that a particular car was so carefully built and tested that it was almost unknown for it to develop a fault, and that it was necessary to take it in for greasing only every five thousand miles, would pay handsome dividends. If it were also possible for the advertisement truthfully to state that all greasing could be done by the owner in half an hour on Saturday morning, without recourse to a pit and without getting dirty, I am not sure that the car wouldn't become an overnight best-seller! But perhaps that is too much to expect.

Now back to this small-car project, a project which must necessarily be hedged in by so many ifs and buts at this theoretical stage that the final formula is screened behind a haze of doubt.

However, I am going to indulge myself to the extent of allowing the design team plenty of time and plenty of money for development. So we are therefore starting with very few preconceived notions, and little more than basic principles.

For example, I should not commit us to front-wheel drive, although I am strongly prejudiced in its favour, without trying it out first. In a small car there are distinct drawbacks, particularly with regard to the gearbox. Ideally this should be out ahead of the engine, as in the Citroen, but this is dimensionally wasteful. But which ever way the engine is placed a spur gear has to be used. In the Citroen the noise this creates is muffled by the intervening engine. In the Mini–Minor it creates a noise nuisance which Issigonis for all his brilliance has not entirely resolved.

One is the question of transmission noise, another is the positioning of the front wheels. In spite of the smallest wheels ever fitted to a motor car, their intrusion into the front compartment of the Mini-Minor is a nuisance and demands an awkward and unnaturally oblique driving position if one is rather large and rather old. We should, then, keep our minds open about front-wheel drive until we had worked on it quite a bit.

My mind would, however, remain firmly and negatively closed on two further points: I would firstly be strongly opposed to placing the engine at the rear of the car. It is a bad position, it is inconvenient (limiting luggage space and the interior heating system among other things) and potentially dangerous in the sort of crisis which can be resolved simply and safely by the average driver with a front-engined car. I know it is possible to point out that millions of rear-engined Volkswagens, Renaults and Fiats have been sold in the past ten years, but I cannot believe that the vast new demand that they have filled all over the world would not have been equally satisfied with a front-engined vehicle with twice the luggage space, a higher safety factor, increased rear leg-room, and so on.

Of course, for ninety-nine per cent of drivers for ninety-nine per cent of the time there is little real danger in a rear-engined car. The vice in them is shown up only on occasion when they are driven to the limit, or in certain critical situations.

I am thankful that this country has at last exposed the myth of rear-engine superiority, a myth originating of course from the success of the Volkswagen. But it is not the position of the engine that has gained for this German car its high reputation. This reputation has been acquired in spite of the disadvantageous siting of the unit.

My second negative is swing-axle rear suspension, which I do not care for because the wheels move in an arc, giving you more trouble with steering on the straight. This is a vexed and highly complicated question, I know, and I do not propose to go into it in any detail here.

The 'oversteer' and its potential dangers created by a rear-placed engine and swing-axle suspension can of course be reduced and 'faked up', and in the case of some cars, like the German Porsche, the faking has been cleverly done. But it is still fundamentally an unsound layout to my mind and I wouldn't want to have anything to do with it.

I don't think we should start off with any preconceived notions about suspension, except of course that it should be independent at the front. The use of coil or torsion bars would be determined in the layout, whichever works into the design better. At the rear I would not use a live axle, and the bevel gearbox and brakes would be in one with the chassis, so that torque reaction would be taken through the frame instead of tending to lift the offside wheel.

So there it is in outline and hedged in by imponderables: the new British small car that will—perhaps mercifully—never even reach the drawing-board.

I was only day-dreaming, anyway.

5

. . . and the Bentleys That Never Were

In the last chapter I talked in very vague and general terms, and prospectively, about the purely academic subject of a new small Bentley motor car. Continuing on this abstract and rather nebulous note, I want to say a few words, retrospectively, about some of the Bentleys that nearly were; not, I hasten to add, because I think any lessons can be learnt from them, but purely for what this information is worth to those interested in speculation. As this book has no hidden motives and is mainly intended as light entertainment, this seems a good enough reason to mention these ghost cars from the past.

I only wish I could remember more about them. My memory is not as good as it was; all the notes and drawings have been lost in the course of house moves, and no one else seems to remember much about them; although Charles Sewell, who worked with me on pretty well every project we tackled, still has a few details.

The first 'ghost' was the car we worked on for Napiers at the Bentley works in 1931. It was, I think, to have been called, appropriately if not originally, the Napier-Bentley. This car, which I mentioned in my autobiography, was to have been the next natural stage in development of the 8-litre Bentley, of which only some one hundred were built. There was, of course, never the opportunity to work much on the original 8-litre, so we naturally welcomed the opportunity of carrying on while

[61]

the company was in the hands of the Official Receiver. (Was this, I wonder, the only car to be conceived and designed under these somewhat unusual circumstances?) I had always liked Napier products, from those magnificent great pre-1914 machines which Edge publicized so cleverly, until their last rather ponderous but beautifully made 40-50 model made in the 'twenties. Napier's high standing, and the fact that in future it seemed as if we would be associated with the company, did help to offset in some degree the disappointment we had all felt at the winding-up of the old firm.

Napiers gave us every possible assistance and encouragement until Rolls-Royce put a stop to it all when they bought Bentley Motors. The car had a single overhead camshaft six-cylinder engine, with four valves per cylinder, and had 'square' dimensions of 110 × 110 mm, giving a capacity of just over 6¼ litres. It was in some respects a scaled-down 8-litre, but the crankshaft was completely redesigned and made more robust; and it revved at a good deal higher speed than the older car. There was nothing very revolutionary about the chassis, which was both lighter and shorter than the earlier car's, and we used semi-elliptics all round for the suspension, although to achieve a lower floor level we dropped the frame after the front axle. This, with the shorter wheelbase and a general lightening all round, made it an altogether lighter car than the 8-litre.

Incidentally, Sewell told me only recently that he was a member of a team that almost got into production with another car which, on paper at least, would have been very interesting. This also had a single overhead camshaft, with inclined valves, and was a high-performance six-cylinder engine of 4 litres, 85 × 115 mm. Other features of this further aborted Napier were four valves per cylinder, two S.U. carburettors, a detachable head and a gross output of 120 b.h.p. which was to have propelled this 35-cwt. machine at an estimated 90 m.p.h. It was to have had a very rigid deep frame to combat the menace of flexibility that so many big cars suffered at that time, and very long semi-elliptic springs.

My 8-litre at Cannes

'Babe' Barnato's impressive 8-litre, with the Hon. Mrs Victor Bruce,
who had just run twenty-four hours at Montlhery at 89·5 m.p.h. on a
4½-litre Bentley. Bernard Rubin is in the back seat

The mammoth
V16 Cadillac

12 h.p. f.w.d. Citroen

Early Hillman Minx, the first
car I bought after the end of
Bentley Motors

Post-war stop-gap,
1946 Standard 8 at Menton

It certainly sounds a most interesting car. Apparently they worked on it for three years, and then Napiers were obliged to put it into cold storage owing to the sudden pressure of re-armament orders at the beginning of 1935.

Incidentally, criticism is sometimes made of the great strength and weight of many of the chassis produced in the late 'twenties and early 'thirties, but it must be remembered that these were usually designed to take coachbuilt bodies to the customers' own tastes. These requirements rarely took much account of weight, and the coachbuilders could never tell what the total weight of the body would be until it was completed. The result was, sometimes, appallingly high; thus the designers' conservatism.

Just ten years later, in the closing stages of a war that had naturally 'killed' the V12 Lagonda car, and when the demand for new armament projects was subsiding, our minds naturally turned to a future car programme. I mention the 2½-litre else-where in this book, but it was our intention to augment this semi-luxury high-performance car with something smaller and cheaper. The size and production facilities of the Lagonda Company had increased tremendously since 1939, and it was now possible to contemplate quite large-quantity production of a cheap small car. This was something I had wanted to do for a long time, and the prospect excited me.

Early in 1945, therefore, we set about two exercises for possible future planning. For the basic formula of the first of these we went back thirty years to another world war, and to the B.R. rotary aero engines, which were perhaps the most successful and certainly the most satisfying engines for which I was responsible.

I had been much impressed by the front-wheel drive Citroen design of 1934, and had driven one of these cars for many thousands of miles. The merits of driven front wheels in a small car are obvious, allowing a high safety factor com-bined with economy of space. I was convinced at that time that the future of the small car lay in the principle of the engine being over or adjacent to the driven wheels, and, with the immediate rejection as bad layout of the rear engine, we had to decide on the best transmission arrangement, bearing in mind the prerequisite that as much weight as possible must bear down on the front wheels for maximum adhesion and controllability.

There were two obvious lessons to be learnt: from the f.w.d. Alvis of the 'twenties, a remarkably advanced design by the distinguished Captain Smith-Clarke, and the Citroen itself. The Alvis suffered from the disadvantage of having the engine and gearbox too far back in the chassis, and the consequent weight distribution made them tricky cars and unpredictable to handle.

The Citroen, of course, had (and has to this day) the engine sensibly placed right over the front wheels, but this led to transmission complications with the gearbox out (very vulnerably) in front and driving back to the axle.

By combining aircraft-engine practice with the benefits of front-wheel drive I thought we might be able to learn some valuable lessons, and perhaps even get some way along the road towards the ideal small car. We therefore worked on a five-cylinder radial engine driving vertically down on to the front wheels. This was to be a very light unit with an aluminium head, air-cooled, with a cowled-in fan forcing the air on to the finned cylinders. The valves were to be inclined, operated by pushrods, and the cam gear followed Bentley Rotary engine practice, which itself was based on Clerget principles.

The combustion chambers were hemispherical, the pistons aluminium—in fact, the heaviest single component was the flywheel, which was necessarily quite substantial. Transmission was through an all-synchromesh gearbox. Originally I think the cylinder dimensions were to have been 63×72 mm, but we later enlarged these to $72 \times 69\frac{1}{2}$ mm; a slightly over-square engine with a capacity of some 1360 c.c. and an R.A.C. rating at that time of 15 h.p.

We knew from the beginning that this would have been a

very refined engine, and with a high power output in relation to its size and especially its weight.

We also recognized that the balance problem would be quite tricky, and we therefore mounted it very flexibly, using a great deal of rubber. In practice the vibrations and the harmonic balance due to the very lightness of the engine were something of a headache. I have no doubt that we should have got round these drawbacks, given time, but we shelved this radial and continued the exercise on an entirely different level, intending to come back to it again if we did not succeed better with the new concept.

In retrospect I think this would have been a very good or a very bad car!

We worked next on an air-cooled flat-six. Although the layout was entirely different, of course, to the radial, the size and pattern were similar, and light weight was again to be achieved by using aluminium cylinders and pistons, and an aluminium head. The six cylinders were horizontally opposed, with the many advantages that this layout combined.

In addition, we arranged the transmission on the Citroen principle with the gearbox out in front driving back to the bevel-box. This allowed us to raise the centre line of the engine and obtain reasonable accessibility, which can sometimes be a difficulty with horizontally opposed engines, as those who have had a Jowett Javelin will know.

We thought at the time we were on to something original with the flat-six, but someone must have been working on the same lines, for very shortly after this a successful flat-six lightweight aero engine appeared in America.

The flat-six was to have had torsion-bar independent front suspension, but, like the Citroen, we thought a beam axle would be preferable at the rear, as without bevel-box drive shafts, etc., it would give us a lower unsprung weight. It would also be cheaper and lighter. In this case we could see no immediate benefit in having full independence.

Two considerations prompted us to put aside the flat-six,

too, and concentrate wholly on the more orthodox $2\frac{1}{2}$-litre car. The first was our lack of facilities at Lagondas, which would have made the development both of this and the radial designs a long business, longer perhaps than the company could afford if we were not to miss the sudden tremendous demand for a small car that would be unleashed at the end of hostilities.

But I think we were also a little nervous about transmitting so much power through the front wheels, for the output of both engines was to have been quite high in relation to the intended weight of the car. Cord's experience with their front-driven machines influenced us, too. I had heard quite a number of disturbing stories about the handling of the Cord, and difficulties with the steering. Wheel-spin when accelerating hard with this car was also, I believe, something of a problem. Perhaps, we decided, this was a gamble we should not take after all.

But I don't think the few months we spent on these two designs were wasted as a great deal of interesting information came to light, and everyone concerned with them learnt many useful lessons.

There have been many other 'ghosts', of course, some of which have scarcely reached the doodling-on-drawing-board stage. A good design team is constantly working on experimental projects or exercises, many of which, like the eight-cylinder engine and other ideas we worked on at Lagondas for a time, never get beyond the discussion or preliminary drawing stage. Stagnation is the great enemy which must be held at bay, and even the most impractical ideas act as stimulants.

6

Some Motoring Men

Dᴜʀɪɴɢ more than fifty years in the motor world I have met quite a number of the leading people connected in one way or another with it, and of course in the racing field pretty well everyone connected with the sport from organizers to drivers, team managers to mechanics.

This has been a pleasant experience, for which I am grateful, because I think on the whole that the motor business, at least in my time, included as friendly and interesting a lot of men as any other branch of industry or commerce. With almost all of them I got on well—manufacturers, designers, salesmen; although perhaps I ought to qualify this because I must confess to having had a little difficulty from time to time with some of the bigger men in the business hailing from the Midlands. The least said about several of them the better; so I will in fact say nothing.

I think among the really big men William Morris (whom we now know, of course, as Lord Nuffield) was at once the most remarkable and unremarkable. I first met him sometime in the winter of 1925-6, I think, under rather difficult circumstances.

The Bentley Company was desperate for money and I took upon myself the unhappy task of trying to find somebody who would take a financial interest in the production of comparitively expensive and rather specialist motor cars in a time of industrial gloom and an imminent General Strike.

I had already tried quite a number of people without any success when I wrote to him asking for an appointment. On a pleasant winter's day I drove down to see him in a very new 6½-litre Bentley, with which I hoped to impress him. At this time Morris was producing a small range of what he will not mind my calling good, cheap, well-made and eminently saleable motor cars. There was the, to some, immortal bull-nosed Cowley, selling at that time at £170 ranging up to a de-luxe, four-cylinder Oxford at £260.

It was my aim to convince him that it would be good business to branch out into a more exotic and exciting field.

I went straight to his office—a pleasant, modest, little private house, which I suppose had once stood more or less on its own but was already by then surrounded by his vast works. I believe, by the way, that the house is still there today.

I recognized him at once as a complete contrast both in appearance and character to the popular conception of the loud, bustling, extravagantly phrased, successful industrialist. With Morris there was none of this barking down a multitude of telephones, restless pacing of the floor and 'big talk' that might be expected of one in his position. When Morris talked it was at a practical down-to-earth level, modestly phrased and with never a wasted word; and his appearance might be des-scribed as that, say, of a legal clerk dedicated to his calling and determined to do well in it.

Certainly no one meeting him in the street would have associated him in any way with engineering, and I have never met a more un-tycoonish tycoon.

I think Morris probably recognized that he had been rather fortunate in being, as the saying goes, at the right time at the right place with the right skill. He had put on the market the sort of car that everyone was crying out for and he had both the courage to back his opinion and the means to deliver the goods. What I think really elevated him to millionairedom was his sound financial judgment in avoiding going to the City for his money. Unlike almost everyone else at that time, he succeeded in avoiding taking on big loans from the merchant bankers, insurance companies, etc. It was the most astute move he ever made and enabled him to make the enormous personal fortune for which he was to become famous.

Morris seemed quite relaxed when I met him that day, in spite of the tremendously long hours he worked and the worries and responsibilities he must have been carrying. He struck me as a very genuine, nice man. After we had talked for a while he took me round a part of the works and I remember being greatly impressed by what I saw, which was indeed in very striking contrast with our little works.

After that I took him out in the 6½-litre. He said many pleasant things about the car, but although he was non-committal about the possibility of taking a financial interest in us I was left with the impression that he didn't think it would work. Later, he wrote a very courteous letter, saying that he didn't think he could successfully market both a cheap car for the masses and an expensive sporting motor car. Some years later, of course, he must have changed his mind, for he bought successively the expensive Wolseley and the sporting Riley firms.

I can't imagine a more different character to the steady William Morris, with his quiet, domestic life with his wife, than the vivid and exotic Louis Coatalen.

Louis Herve Coatalen, born in Brittany in 1879, had left France for England in 1901 to join the Crowden Motor Company after working at the drawing-board with Panhard, Clement and De Dion Bouton. He transferred his services to the Humber Company a few months later, where he produced two of the few mundane (but highly successful) cars in his long career, the 8/10 and 10/12. A few years later he was invited to become Chief Designer to Hillman, where he soon, and sensibly, married the Chairman's daughter and produced a lively little machine in the Hillman-Coatalen. I first met Coatalen when we were staying at the same hotel in Douglas in the Isle of Man for the 1914 Tourist Trophy Race, some five years after he began his long association with Sunbeam. He took me along to see the Sunbeam team cars, and when I commented that he had a good chance of winning with his Peugeots he took it in good part.

One of Coatalen's most endearing qualities was his absence of illusions about himself. Later on he looked at our own single little D.F.P. we had rashly entered for the T.T. and he was more charitable about this car than I had been about his. In the course of the following two days over which the race was run Kenelm Lee Guinness (who described the car as 'a wonderful production') took the first of the Sunbeam cars through to first place at a creditable average speed of 56 m.p.h. on the mountainous circuit.

I think Coatalen would accept the fact that he was not a great designer, but he had many of the characteristics of a first-rate designer, including intelligence and the ability to learn from the lessons of others. In fact this second characteristic was so highly developed that if his cars were beaten by, say, a Peugeot or a Fiat, he would at once contrive to obtain the services of the man responsible for those cars. This may have been a short-cut and even drastic way of doing things, but it worked.

Coatalen was also quite enough of an engineer to know why others followed certain lines in their design, and to be able to benefit from their example and even improve on it. This aptitude is, of course, something that every good designer must have, be he a Henry Royce or an Ernest Henri.

Coatalen was not only a first-class business man who made (and lost) a great deal of money in his active life with Sunbeams; he had other qualities which I liked even better; he was highly amusing and a tremendous raconteur, and he was dedicated to motor racing. He drove at Brooklands in the very early days, in other people's cars which he tuned up himself to go very fast, and he was quite a successful driver.

Coatalen managed to produce some remarkably fast Hillmans when he was with that firm, but his big chance came when he got the post of Chief Designer at Sunbeams. They were producing at that time a series of sound sloggers, and although through the years that he was with Sunbeams he never succeeded in persuading them to discard their 'bread-and-butter', he at once set to work on the competition side, producing first a four-cylinder, 96 × 135 mm car and then a 12/16 h.p. in 1911, which, in stripped form, had some success in competitions. Coatalen's first pure racing machine, named *Nautilus* after his fellow countryman's fantastic underwater craft in *20,000 Leagues Under the Sea*, had a special 92 × 160 mm engine with four valves per cylinder and twin overhead cam-shafts. This was followed by *Toodles II*, another single-seater, which had a series of wins at Brooklands in 1911. His 16/20 and six-cylinder 25/30-h.p. models sold well as touring cars to the public, and in modified form did well in racing.

Later came the Peugeot-derived sixteen-valve 3·3-litre cars, very stark racing machines, which easily won the 1914 T.T. and did the firm's reputation a lot of good; and of course the G.P. Sunbeam of 1922 which, in spite of its obvious Italian derivation, achieved Britain's first Grand Prix win and brought this country great prestige.

I have no knowledge of Coatalen's relationship with Sunbeams during these years but I have a feeling that sometimes he must have had to use all his considerable powers of persuasion to allow him to use so much of the Company's resources in racing.

We came up against Sunbeams on few occasions and they never really worried us in competition. I remember Coatalen brought a team of 3-litre Sunbeams to Le Mans in 1925 and although it was a disastrous year for us and Chassagne and Sammy Davis brought one of the cars into second place among the Lorraines, we were quite as fast as they were before our troubles started.

Outside motor racing I saw something of Coatalen during World War I when I was at the Admiralty. Among other things it was my job to convince him of the merits of the aluminium piston which we had first used, with surprising results, in the D.F.P. Like everyone else, Coatalen had no idea what had made the D.F.P. travel so quickly, and it did not take me long to convince him of its superiority for aero engines. 'You're a very good salesman, W.O.,' he said at the conclusion of our talk; and this was about the most flattering thing a salesman supreme could have said to someone who had no illusions about his commercial acumen.

During the course of the war Sunbeams had the distinction of producing a greater variety of aero engines than any other firm, in part because Coatalen was so good at selling ideas to the Admiralty and the War Office.

Soon afterwards Coatalen became almost obsessed with simple out-and-out speed for speed's sake, and by marrying the 18-litre V12 Sunbeam 'Manitou' aero engine, modified to produce 335 horsepower, with a monstrous chassis, on several occasions acquired the World Land Speed Record with K. Lee Guinness and Malcolm Campbell at the wheel. In the eyes of some people this may well have been meritorious, but I am afraid I have always thought that cars built for this purpose only are of no practical value and a perversion of good engineering. In my opinion, land-speed-record attempts are made as stunts, as spectacles or for profit, or all three. But I know I am in a minority about this and am probably wrong.

The 1914 T.T. was quite a social affair and as there were a number of practice sessions followed by a race that lasted two days, the entrants, drivers, manufacturers and mechanics had plenty of time to get to know one another. I met a number of people besides Coatalen and renewed old friendships with others.

Among these was Laurence H. Pomeroy. His apprenticeship period, like mine, was spent with locomotives and he spent some time with a firm of civil engineers and with the Thornycroft Company at Basingstoke before going to the design department of Vauxhall Motors in 1906. His first car there was a four-cylinder car (90 mm × 120 mm), which I believe did very well in tuned form at Brooklands, and in modified form became the luxury tourer 'Prince Henry', which was still in production when the first 30/98 Vauxhall appeared in 1913. Pomeroy left Vauxhall's in 1920, worked for a time in America, and later became Managing Director of the Daimler Company.

Like Coatalen, Laurence H. Pomeroy was an excellent and an amusing talker and a good man to have on the platform or as guest speaker at a dinner. He was, I believe, a very good lecturer and read learned papers with fluency and humour. Pomeroy had wide technical knowledge and technical flair, and he was very widely educated in all aspects of engineering.

As a practical designer he was perhaps rather less successful. While he remained loyal to the orthodox he produced some very sound motor cars, but if he delved experimentally into the unorthodox the results were not always quite so happy. But there are few designers remembered for producing two such excellent motor cars as the Prince Henry Vauxhall and the 30/98.

On the subject of Vauxhalls, by the way, of which the 30/98 was, I suppose, our closest rival in the 'twenties, it was interesting to hear the reports of owners who had shifted allegiance to the 3-litre Bentley. After the Vauxhall's bigger engine, of course, they noticed the rather inferior acceleration and top speed of the Bentley but they always commented that they could travel faster from point to point over English roads in our car with its superior braking and road-holding. I always thought it would have made a nice car to have put the Vauxhall engine into our chassis. Perhaps someone has even done this.

One of the men I should have much liked to meet but never succeeded in doing so was Marc Birkigt, a great Swiss engineer. Birkigt was born in Geneva in 1878 and, like so many other designers, turned his attention first to locomotives, though in his case to electric locomotives. At the turn of the century he was working in Barcelona where in 1904 he started the Hispano-Suiza factory with French and Spanish financial backing. In the next ten years over thirty different models appeared, culminating in the famous 3·6-litre Alfonso, named after the Spanish monarch. Between the wars such great designs as the 6·2-litre, 37·2-h.p. of 1919, the more sporting 'Monza' and the 'Boulogne' were produced.

I consider that Birkigt had a more profound influence on the development of the internal combustion engine than anyone else. He is, to my mind, one of the very great. Birkigt succeeded above anyone else in being a successful innovator while combining technical knowledge, imagination and a balanced regard for the compromise between orthodoxy and unorthodoxy.

Let me tell a story, which has been both told and denied before, to point my meaning. The Mercedes Company made one of their few serious mistakes in having one of their Grand Prix cars in their Long Acre showrooms when war broke out in 1914. I knew this and immediately told Commander Wilfred Briggs, my chief at the Admiralty, about it. Without wasting any time, we went along to Long Acre and retrieved the hidden car before anyone could destroy it. We then had the engine sent up to Rolls-Royce at Derby who examined, vetted and tested it exhaustively. It is common knowledge that all Rolls-Royce aero engines built during World War I were based quite closely on this engine; in fact, Mercedes is reputed to have sent a facetious invoice to Derby while the war was at its height demanding a royalty share; but that is doubtless an apocryphal story.

The real secret behind the success of the Rolls-Royce Eagle aero engine of World War I was in the cooling and arrangement of their cylinders, in the design of the cylinders themselves, and, of course, as in all R-R products, in the detail design and workmanship which made them wonderfully reliable. The V12, 1240-cu. in. engine had cylinders machined from steel forgings and spherical-shaped combustion chambers in which the valves were seated in the heads and surrounded by thin steel water jackets, also welded. This design gave excellent and really efficient cooling.

This may have been quite heavy and also expensive to manufacture but it represented a great advance, and accounted for the superiority of many of the Rolls-Royce aero engines during World War I, which in some of their final series were producing up to 400 b.h.p. Later on, Renault followed the same practice with their aero engines.

This was a great step in aero-engine design, but it was Birkigt who was responsible for the next, and very much more important, stage—a stage which marks what I consider to be one of the greatest forward advances in the design of the aero engine.

It was Birkigt who produced in the spring of 1916 his famous V8 aero engine, which incorporated a number of patented design features. The cylinders were formed from an aluminim block with cored water passages into which were screwed four forged-steel barrels, threaded on the outside and closed at the top. Gas passages were formed in the aluminium and the valves were seated on the steel head. The pistons also were of aluminium. The valves were seated vertically in the cylinder head along the centre of each block, operated directly by a single overhead camshaft supported by three plain bronze bearings and driven by a vertical driveshaft and bevel gears.

Among the firms who produced this excellent engine under licence (Wolseley, Simplex and Wright-Martin were others) was the Napier company, and towards the end of World War I they went one better and added a further bank of cylinders to the Hispano-based design, which became the 'W' type Napier Lion. Even in its earliest form the Lion produced 500 b.h.p., and it was so good that it virtually wiped out Rolls-Royce's lead in aero engines. Among its numerous achievements, these engines powered many of Malcolm Campbell's *Bluebird* record-breaking cars, and they had the distinction of providing the motive power of John Cobb's car which to this day, forty years later, still holds the World Land Speed Record.

Later, of course, Rowledge, who had been the brains behind the Lion engine, was invited to join the Rolls-Royce company; and in due course, with the aluminium Merlin engine, R-R regained the lead before World War II broke out.

All this may be a side issue, but it is not really irrelevant if it underlines again Birkigt's enormous importance and influence in the field of design.

Birkigt's V8 aero engine alone would have ensured his inclusion among the great twentieth-century engineers. But there was much else besides for he was a true innovator. He was, for example, using servo-assisted four-wheel brakes on his 37·2-h.p., six-cylinder car while many other luxury or high-performance cars still had brakes on the rear wheels only.

It was a tragedy that economic conditions, combined with the political situation, forced Birkigt to give up motor-car design by the mid-1930s, when the French factory was turned over to armaments and the Spanish works sold to Pegaso. If the brain of this genius had remained, until his death in 1953, wholly devoted to the motor car, there is no doubt in my mind that the internal combustion engine would by now have reached an even higher state of development.

The reference to Rolls-Royce a few pages back seems to make this an appropriate place to say a few words about Ernest Walter Hives, who at one time had a considerable influence on my life.

I mentioned in my autobiography my very great regard and admiration for Lord Hives, who must be more responsible than any other single man for the unique position that Rolls-Royce holds today in British industry and engineering.

Lord Hives is a thick-set, heavily built man, now seventy-four years old, whom I remember chiefly for his shrewd twinkling eyes and delightful sense of humour. He is neither a snob nor an inverted snob but a man-of-the-world anti-snob, and a gentleman in the best meaning of the word.

I first met Hives in World War I when I was at the Admiralty and he had just been put in charge of the Experimental Department at Derby. Before this he had been employed by Rolls-Royce since 1908 in the Design and Experimental Department, and among other things had co-driven on the famous non-stop run in top gear from London to Edinburgh and back on a Silver Ghost, had driven in the Six-Day Trial, and had driven a stripped, high-geared Rolls-Royce round Brooklands at a three-figure lap speed.

Hives's work in the Experimental Department was so outstanding that it at once became apparent that he was destined for great things. And so, of course, he was.

Without Hives there would have been no Merlin engines to power the Spitfires and Hurricanes in the Battle of Britain, and Operation Sea-Lion, for the invasion of Britain, could not only have taken place but might well have proved successful. Hives's genius was not as a creative designer but as a redesigner. His brilliance lay, in short, in taking a design and making it work, and above all in interpreting in practical form the general instructions of Henry Royce. His patience, persistence, his conscientiousness and obstinacy, all combined to provide him with a temperament ideally suited to his role as a development engineer. From a basically sound design that was still bristling with faults he would produce over months and even years of painstaking endeavour an engine that provided great power with satisfactory reliability. I can't help thinking, too, that his sense of humour contributed greatly towards his success.

Calmness was another of Hives's invaluable assets. I remember being at Derby one day when development on the Merlin was at its height and catastrophe had followed catastrophe. One of the engines was on the bed at the time, and while I was talking to Hives a man burst excitedly into the room and told him in horror-struck tones that it had blown up again. 'I see,' remarked Hives quietly, sparing the man nothing more than a courteous glance.

In addition to this unique combination of qualities, which

would have taken him to the top of the technical tree anyway, Hives had the judgment and mental balance which make a good administrator. For me it was a privilege and an education to watch him at work. Rolls-Royce will probably never have anyone like him again.

Sir Henry Royce has been the subject of greater veneration than Lord Hives will probably ever receive. But I personally place Royce on a quite different and even on a lower plane. Perhaps this is a personal prejudice that should not be taken too seriously. I admired Royce's attention to detail—his obsession for perfectly fitting door locks and superlative controls and switches—very much. I completely accept the fact that his standards of workmanship were probably higher than those of anyone else in the whole age of the motor car. But I don't think that his main *designs* were in any way outstanding. I am not being in the least disparaging of Henry Royce when I repeat what has long been accepted by many people: that he was not a creator. In fact it is said that his chief claim was that he would take the designs of other people and improve them beyond all expectations of the originators. That was the whole basis of his design philosophy—and there are many worse!

Henry Royce's early training and mine were very similar. We had both been interested in locomotives as boys and we both worked as apprentices for the Great Northern Railway, although Royce was at Peterborough some years before I was at Doncaster. He started in the motor business after buying a French car, running it carefully for some time while keeping it under observation for faults so that he would not repeat the same mistakes in his own first car.

The first experimental two-cylinder Royce, admirable and historic machine as it certainly was, included no feature of any originality. The same can be said of every Rolls-Royce car produced in the succeeding fifty years. Royce was not interested in originality, nor in the broad outline of the design, which often contained fundamental faults, although not of course in the workmanship. Workmanship in design and construction,

The V12 Lagonda at Brooklands in 1939: Le Mans car in the foreground, my own saloon behind

Four-door saloon with body by Lagonda

Pit stop at Le Mans in 1939

The Cricklewood
works as first built
about 1920

Eight years later

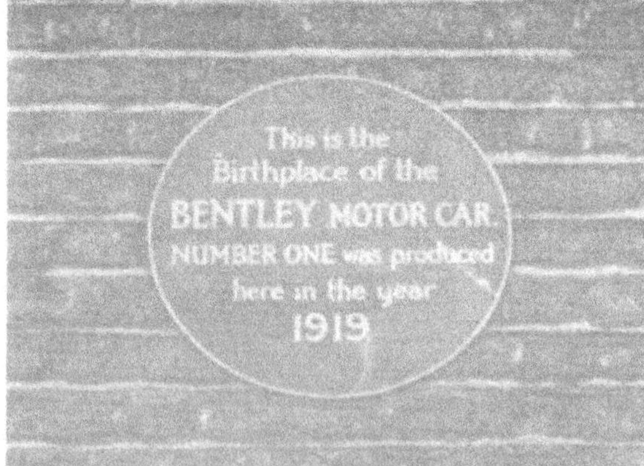

The plaque The Bentley
Drivers' Club placed
on the wall of New Street
Mews off Baker Street,
which can be seen today

and immense care in assembly, are now generally accepted as the secrets of the astonishing success and long life of all the Rolls-Royce cars built prior to World War II. In broad outline of design every Rolls-Royce car can be said to have looked backwards for its inspiration. The 20-h.p. model of 1922, for example, was really a Buick in essence, suitably de-tuned for reliability and silence, and with vastly better detail work; and the 'new' aluminium V8 engine which has justly been highly praised is a type often used in America.

It was characteristic of Royce's philosophy that he was not very interested in the ease of servicing and cleaning the engine and mechanics of his motors. But this failing (if failing it is) did, in fact, have serious results, for in the days when the Rolls-Royce Company was struggling to establish itself as the producer of the ultimate in motor transportation for the rich, it was the family chauffeurs who were most responsible for the selection of their masters' or mistresses' cars. In many households their word was law on all motoring matters. And chauffeurs did not care very much for the Rolls-Royce because, in an age when the sparkling cleanliness of the engine compartment was regarded as at least equally important to the shine on the brass and paintwork, the Rolls-Royce engine was a devil to clean, service and maintain.

In those Edwardian days it was the Daimler Knight engine which was regarded as the nearest to perfection by the all-powerful chauffeurs. The Daimler engine with its big sleeve valves also provided the superlative silence so highly esteemed by the Edwardian chauffeur and his master and mistress. In addition the 57-h.p. Daimler performed quite as well as the Silver Ghost.

Henry Royce tackled these two problems with characteristic vigour and thoroughness. He got over the problem of noise (though lack of complete silence is the better term) by working away on the tappets and accuracy and design of camshafts. Then Claude Johnson, the administrative brain behind the early years of the Rolls-Royce Company's life, softened up the sales resistance with a very subtle move by opening a sort of chauffeurs' training college, at which those who were to be responsible for the maintenance of their charges were given a thoroughly pleasant, and flattering, fortnight's course. By 1914 every decent family who could afford one had a Rolls-Royce, and Lanchester were running a poor second, with Daimlers third.

I only met Royce once or twice, under rather unhappy circumstances, and I wish I had got to know him better.

Another man I should have enjoyed knowing better was Georges Roesch. In fact I think we talked together only once, which can be explained by the fact that we were both very preoccupied during our most active years as designers. It is surprising how many outstanding designers the Swiss have produced. Roesch was another. Like Birkigt, he was born in Geneva. He worked for a time under Louis Renault in Paris, and, after a time with Daimlers, joined that strange, loosely tied empire of Sunbeam-Talbot-Darracq. Then at some time around 1924 he became chief designer of Talbots in London and produced that excellent middle-size, middle-performing car, the 14/45. From that sprang the range of Talbot models which continued right up to the Rootes take-over in 1935. These cars performed very well, on the roads as well as in competition, and included many mechanical innovations.

Roesch never produced a bad car and his last 105 model Talbot was a very good car indeed, and very fast. He was a clever and ingenious designer, but perhaps sometimes he was a shade too clever and complex, as anyone who has tried to overhaul the engine of a Talbot 75 will agree. I think, too, that the men at the foundry who cast the heads for Roesch cars might have had something to say about his occasional tortuous extravagances and complexities, not all of which seemed justified by results. But the Roesch Talbots of 1925–35 played a very important part in the history of the motor car between the two world wars, and a well-preserved model is always a rewarding sight on the roads today.

I was very grieved to read recently of the death of Harry Ferguson. This clever Irishman always had a great interest in our cars in the Bentley Motors days, and he was often in the pits at Brooklands and at the Ulster Tourist Trophy races, following our progress with enthusiasm and lending a hand whenever he could. He was for a long time our agent in Belfast and sold a good number of cars, but it was a tragedy that he never quite succeeded in applying his theoretical brilliance in practical terms. He did, of course, do a lot in the world of agricultural machinery, made the tractor much safer, and made a vast fortune out of Fords of America. Congenial company as I always found him, I believe he was not very easy to work with. It remains to be seen whether anything comes of his widely publicized yet highly secret experiments with suspension and traction which were still going on at the time of his death.

Ever since it appeared in 1949 I have owned a succession of Morris Minors, a useful, sensible and thoroughly practical motor car for British roads today. I don't know what would have happened to Nuffield before the 1952 amalgamation with Austin had it not been for the Minor, which for twelve years had a waiting list, and, so far as I know, was the only Morris car to have made a sensible profit after the war.

The designer of the Morris Minor was, of course, Alec Issigonis, now famous and the subject of praise from all over the world for the Mini-Minor. Issigonis was born in Smyrna in 1906 and came to England at the age of sixteen to study engineering at London University. His first interest, I believe, has always been in suspension, and this has been reflected in the work he did for Morris's, which he joined in 1936, from the pre-war cars right down to the extraordinary 'rubber sprung' Mini-Minor. He was four years away from B.M.C. when he completed designs for Alvis of a $3\frac{1}{2}$-litre V8 car which was to incorporate a form of hydraulic suspension. I first met Issigonis at Epsom Golf Club in 1949 just after I had bought my first side-valve Minor, and have met him at Oxford on several occasions. I have always liked him very much as a man and found him good company.

As a designer I admire particularly his down-to-earth approach to problems. He puts mathematics and theory in their proper place and sets about the design of a new car in an admirably straightforward manner, and with a very clear picture in his mind of what he wants to do. He always gets straight down to practical engineering. It is now well known that he intended the Minor to have a flat-four engine, which accounts for the wide front track that has been more responsible than anything else for the car's excellent road-holding and cornering. But I believe there were some difficulties with this engine, and instead the old pre-war Morris 8 engine was used.

The Minor was produced at astonishing speed, like the later Mini-Minor, and its success took Nuffield by surprise. Having completed the Minor, Issigonis went to Alvis after the Austin-Morris merger and stayed there until B.M.C., who were perhaps conscious of a certain sterility in their design department, persuaded him to come back. Issigonis returned on his own terms, and with a very strong and completely free hand. With the same facility and sympathy with the unorthodox that had produced the Morris Minor he set to work on his new design and, like every good designer, borrowing freely from the best work of others before him, produced what can only be described as a world-beater.

Issigonis recognizes as well as anyone that there is no merit in novelty for novelty's sake. There is nothing novel about front-wheel drive, nor even in the transverse engine of a Mini-Minor, but the combination of the best of both the conventional and unconventional practices of the past, cleverly blended together, have produced a small motor car that is practical, sensible and a pleasure to drive.

I remember telling the Chief Engineer at Nuffields some years ago that Issigonis had produced the near-perfect small motor car for British roads in the Morris Minor but that he should have taken the plunge and insisted on independent suspension at the rear as well as at the front. He laughed good-naturedly at this and said: 'You're just an idealist, and look where idealism got you.'

'All right,' I replied, 'but I'll bet you that all cars, big and small, will have independent rear suspension very soon.'

Nothing pleased me more than to see independent suspension on the rear of the Mini-Minor, and now I suppose four out of five of the world's small cars are independently sprung all round.

I'll conclude this chapter on a few of the more interesting people I have known, or at least brushed up against in the past fifty years, on a personal reminiscence which may or may not carry a moral. It happened at the Bentley Drivers' Club dinner some years ago when I was talking to Sir William Lyons. Lyons, I suppose, can be said to have achieved, while pursuing roughly similar aims as we pursued, the financial success that for many reasons eluded us at Bentley Motors. I like him very much as a man, and I am sure that he has done more than any other single person for the British motor industry. He has also been very astute in refusing to compromise his policy. His cars have always retained their character and their individual feel, and he has never been tempted into producing too many of them. He has also been sensible about racing, never going in for events which he did not feel very confident of winning, and drawing out at the psychological moment when he had learnt all he wanted to learn and gained all the prestige he could hope to gain—and when the benefit of a win was small and the blow of failure was a serious one.

'These affairs must make you feel very proud,' Lyons said as he glanced round the packed banqueting room at the Dorchester.

'But your cars have achieved all that mine did, and a good deal more,' I pointed out.

'But it's not the same thing, you know, not the same thing at all. This sort of thing will never happen again.'

Perhaps Sir William Lyons was right. Perhaps the mystique

that has grown up about the cars we now call 'vintage' will never happen again, now that the romantic period of motoring is behind us. I don't know. But it was a nice thing for Lyons to say, and I appreciated it, just as everything about the Bentley Drivers' Club has given me pleasure and comfort in my retirement.

7

Design and the Designer

I WANT to start this rather diffuse chapter on design in general, and the engines and cars for which I have been responsible in particular, on a slightly defensive note. The reason for this is that, at the time of the 3-litre car and frequently since, people have suggested that I lacked sufficient technical engineering knowledge. It is not my business to defend myself against this charge, but I should like to get this question of technical knowledge into perspective.

It is my belief that nowadays too much stress is laid on the theoretical side of designing, and not nearly enough on its practical side. Perhaps I am prejudiced in this matter, but at the same time I am absolutely certain that in these days too many young men are entering engineering with far too little practical experience. Logarithms, principles of stress and strain and that sort of thing are very well, but there is no substitute for working on the job, up to your elbows in grease, and dressed in overalls rather than a blue suit. It is my belief that you must be absolutely engrossed in the machine, developing almost an obsession for it, and using your hands—as well as your head—in order to get to know what it's all about.

A very long time ago, and before I started my own apprenticeship, I spent a mercifully brief period at King's College in London on theoretical work. I did my best, passed out of the examination and, in due course, and to my everlasting benefit, forgot seventy-five per cent of what I had learnt within a year. I don't think I was a very good pupil at King's. I was slow. I was constantly holding myself back, not because I didn't understand the facts, but because I was constantly asking myself why? why? why? Later, as an apprentice in the works at Doncaster, I was thankful to leave the theory of engineering behind me. I don't know what it is like there today, but fifty years ago it was almost entirely practical work—from the 6 a.m. start until we were dismissed at 5.30 p.m. I used to keep all the technical reading until the evenings.

At Doncaster, as a natural non-mathematician, I was given my head, and by living every day with the machines I learnt from them and became almost a part of them, sometimes thinking out how things could have been improved if one were given the chance to start afresh. In the oil-laden atmosphere of those works, surrounded by the machines which I loved, I began to acquire that engineering sense which is so terribly hard to define but without which I could later have achieved nothing whatever creative in the way of cars, and certainly not the aero engines.

I think it is about as difficult to explain to anyone else this feeling for a machine, this sense almost of comradeship with it, as it is for a gardener to explain away his green fingers or a modern artist to justify his painting. It is my contention that it is as much an art to produce a successful design as any creation in music or painting. The proverbial compromise, the sense of balance and tone, are equally present in, and equally important to, almost any of man's creations.

At Doncaster I acquired a tremendous admiration for Sir Nigel Gresley, who was superintendent of the carriage and wagon works under Ivatt, and was later to become a very young C.M.E. He was one of the greatest locomotive engineers this country has ever produced and, from his early freight engines of 1911, through his early 'Pacific' passenger locomotives to the record-breaking *Mallard*, which travelled at 126 m.p.h. in 1938, Gresley produced numerous fine locomotives.

Gresley's simple philosophy was based on the belief that practical engineering is vastly more important than anything you can learn out of books or directly from others. I began to regret less and less my mathematical incompetence and consoled myself with the knowledge that Gresley was no better than I was at figures, and that he, too, learnt directly from the machine, and so acquired an engineering imagination. I believe I am right in saying of Gresley that the drawing of designs, or working a design out mathematically first, drove him as mad with impatience as it has always exasperated me. With your head close to the drawing-board you can't see anything else at all; it is all detail work and the overall principle of design is liable to be lost.

In my days with the D.F.P. before World War I I don't think I had any particular ambition to produce an engine of my own. Of course, I was encouraged by the success that we had with that car but I was too lacking in experience and confidence to contemplate becoming an original designer. Then, of course, the tempo of everything doubled overnight with the advent of World War I, and in what seems in retrospect as an incredibly short space of time I was working on the B.R.1 aero engine at Gwynne's in Hammersmith. I honestly never expected that engine to come to anything and I was astonished when it went into quantity production and was used to power our fighters in France. I think Zeus was on my side while we were working on the first rotary aero engine.

Consider my position for a moment. I had served an apprenticeship as a locomotive engineer, had fiddled with motor-bicycle engines and taxis, had helped to manage a French motor-car concession for a year or two and had learnt more about the internal-combustion engine as a result of this and of the competition programme we had run. Then I had been swept into the Navy. And now here I was, at the age of twenty-seven, imagining that I was capable of designing an aero engine alongside such 'brains' as Birkigt, Royce, Coatalen, Pomeroy and many others. It was absurd, of course. But this situation was nothing like so extraordinary for me personally as the way the B.R. engine came out just right first time, and at such astonishing speed.

If the B.R. engines had failed, as of course they might so easily have done, then I am sure there would have been no Bentley car. Their immediate success at first caused me delight and astonishment, and then more gradually gave me a feeling of self-confidence. 'I can do this thing,' I can remember telling myself with some surprise. 'It can't be so impossible after all! Perhaps I ought to have another go.'

One reason why the B.R.s worked out the first time, and so quickly, of course, is that with an aero engine one doesn't have to worry about noise—although it is high time now that some attention was paid to this aspect.

Most of our early troubles with the 3-litre engine related to noise, but with the B.R.s this didn't concern us in the least. Simplicity and lightness are the two unique assets of the rotary aero engine. But equalizing the heat round the cylinders was one of the main difficulties to be overcome, as the cylinders had to be made of very thin steel to reduce the centrifugal forces. Earlier rotaries had a sort of bicycle-pump washer called an obturator piston ring, made of alloy, to offset this danger of distortion to the cylinders. But this proved highly unreliable, as I discovered to my cost one day when a French rotary-engined machine in which I was flying packed up in a rainstorm over the south coast, and we had to force-land very roughly in a field. We also finished up just fifteen yards from the cliff-edge.

For the first nine-cylinder B.R. engine we turned to aluminium barrels and pistons with cast-iron liners, which spread the heat equally without the assistance of this dangerous obturator ring, and the B.R.1 mounted in Camel fighters did good work with the R.N.A.S. on the Western Front, the B.R.2 with the R.A.F. as well, in the Snipe.

I have already written in my autobiography about the rotary engines for which I was responsible in World War I, and

I mention them again now only as examples of how things can go almost miraculously right in the design department when luck is on your side, and in spite (in this case) of the urgent necessity for speed.

The bigger 245 b.h.p. B.R.2, which gave our fighters a rate of climb superior to anything the Germans could achieve, worked out equally satisfactorily at even greater speed. The B.R.2 in 1917 was running its fifty-hour Air Ministry acceptance test a fortnight after the prototype engine first turned over and was in quantity production within a few more weeks.

Luck may have been on our side, but I am quite unreasonably proud of those rotary engines; certainly they gave me more satisfaction than any of the car engines we later produced. They had a good power output, and they had that essential quality of reliability because they were so light and never had to be pushed. The B.R.s were always working well within their capacity, and this is something at which I always aimed with the later car engines. A highly stressed power unit has always been anathema for me.

Every six weeks or so during World War I, I went over and watched the aircraft powered by our engines in action over Belgium and to hear direct from the pilots and mechanics of any difficulties they were having. As a result of the enormous satisfaction in hearing from those who flew the machines powered by the B.R. of their superiority over anything the Germans had at the time, I became increasingly confident that I was capable of supervising the design of a motor car, as soon as the war was over. This realization filled me with excitement. I suppose the 3-litre Bentley was born in my mind by 1918.

After what I have written in my autobiography, and earlier in this book, it is hardly necessary for me to stress again that it is a team and not a designer who creates a motor car. I was responsible for the 'design' of the 3-litre Bentley; I was not the designer, neither did I build it. It was a team effort.

For example, at the Humber factory in Coventry I talked over my ideas for a car with F. T. Burgess. Burgess was a sound designer, but not a very adventurous one, and I don't think he would have produced a very interesting design under his own direction. But he was a magnificent draughtsman, the quickest I have ever known, and I could never have carried out the detail work on the drawing-board at which he was so adept. What I wanted was a car that could be driven hard without minding, in the French tradition. I wanted it to be fast and tough, but comfortable and no noisier than it should have been. I saw the 3-litre as a car intended primarily for long-distance motoring, a car with 'long legs' and one that would not let the driver down, for at that time reliability was still a doubtful factor in a touring car.

It was possible in those days to drive long distances at high speed in this country, but it was with a particular eye on Continental roads that the 3-litre was designed. French roads in the 1920s were as straight, and as long, as they are today, but their surface was often appalling and at the same time there was a great temptation to drive fast. What we were aiming at was a car that could be pushed all day long at sixty or more miles an hour over almost any sort of road surface.

Many of the British designs at this time were perfectly all right for local trips and for pottering around. But pressed for any length of time, for perhaps a half-dozen laps round Brooklands at full throttle, and the low top gear and poor cooling would result in burnt-out valves or seized pistons. But the D.F.P. had shown me what could be done, in the French manner. I was determined that the 3-litre should stand up to long punishment, and for this each cylinder should have four valves, not too big, and with water all round for cooling. Equally important was to have water circulating closely round the plugs and cylinders, and, of course, a sensibly high top gear.

At the same time, this car, I decided, should sacrifice none of the merits of the good British touring car of the day. We made no attempt at originality or unorthodoxy in the 3-litre. This was impossible as well as undesirable because we had very little money for experimental work and no development department at all. We knew from the outset that we should have to take the best of what other people had done before us. But we also knew that we must not copy blindly, for that would have been fatal, however good the original product. 'We must take every little bit of every other product,' we told ourselves, 'examine it minutely and ask ourselves: "Why did they do it like this? Why didn't they do it like that?" "Ah yes, they were forced to do this because of so and so. It would have been fatal if they had done anything else." ' In this way we got a fascinating analytical view of the processes of thought that had resulted in a certain design feature in other engines. We simply did the logical thing and took it one stage further.

In the design of the 3-litre two distinguished motor cars influenced us more than any others. These were Henri's 1912 Peugeot and the 1914 Grand Prix Mercedes. I got to know a lot about the Mercedes engine when I used to visit Rolls-Royce at Derby during the war, and was tremendously impressed by it. Our arrangement of the valve gear was rather similar to that used by Mercedes, driving through bevels to a single camshaft. The difference between the Mercedes layout and ours can be seen in these diagrams:

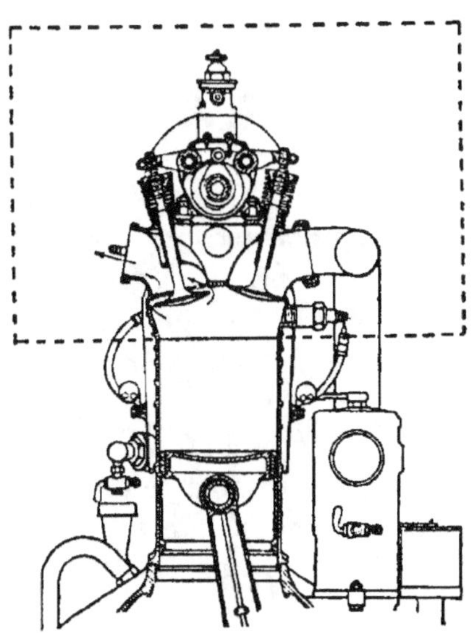

This had the advantage of direct action on the valves without the use of rockers, and the fact that you could put the plug in or near the centre of the crown of the hemispherical combustion space. We should have liked to follow Peugeot with twin overhead camshafts and a valve gear like this:

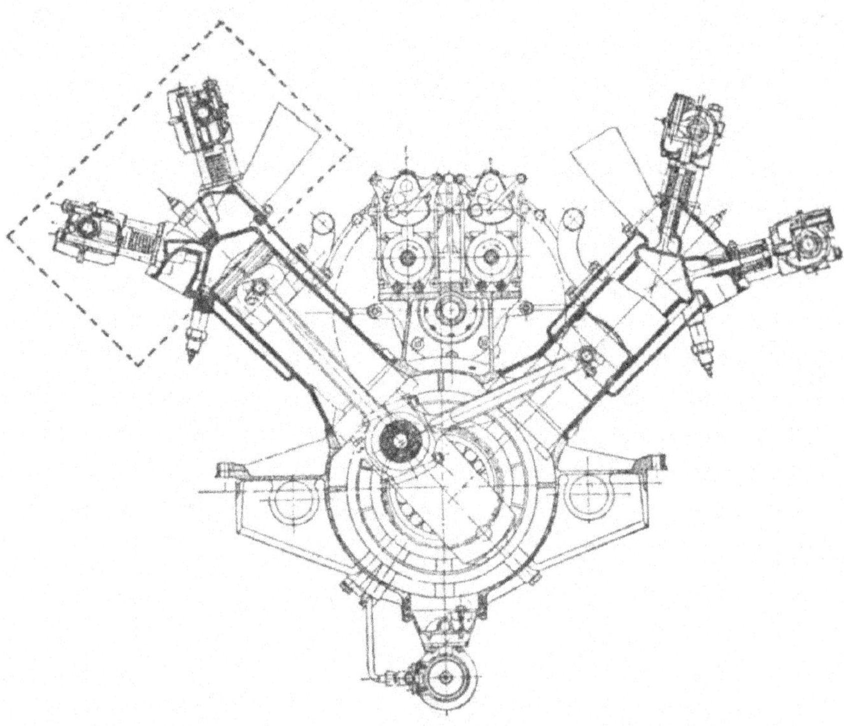

This was both more complicated and more efficient because there was less valve gear reciprocating weight and you could get your plug in the centre. On the debit side, though, two gear-driven camshafts at that time were rather noisy, and we were very conscious of the noise factor in what was to be essentially a touring car. As a result we had to use two plugs, one on each side, to get the same results. Later, more satisfactory camshaft drive methods than the train of gears which always chattered so noisily were discovered, and we felt justified in going back to twin chain-drive o.h.c. with the 2½-litre Lagonda.

Another thing we owed to the Mercedes was the bevel drive to the camshaft. The use of separate steel forgings in the welded-up ports and water jackets was not used, and the design of the cylinder block, which had several cover plates enabling you to be sure that the water passages were clear and free from sand, was our own idea. The lower half of the engine was our own original design, too, for which we owed nothing to anyone.

The gearbox was pretty straightforward, but later we had to supply different ratios for different purposes when people started using the car for work for which it was never intended. Later still, Burgess and I had a go at synchromesh. We used the same principle of frictional synchronization that later became so popular but we never got beyond the sketching stage. We still had no time for development and it would have taken years for just the two of us to get it right with the amount of time we could have devoted to it.

We also toyed at one stage with four-wheel hydraulic brakes. We didn't go as far as the brake shoe; our aim was to get equal pressure on all four wheels and we did work out a self-adjusting arrangement. But we were far too engrossed in other things to be able to spare the time. Instead we had to content ourselves with elaborating the Perrot principle which we eventually adopted.

For suspension, we were quite orthodox, with semi-elliptic front springing and a decent-length back spring for the open propeller shaft. Until the arrival of independent front suspension we suffered in common with everyone else from the limited travel we could allow the front springs.

Mercedes had used a torque tube, Peugeot an open carden shaft which took the torque on the back spring, a principle which we followed.

I have an all too clear memory of my first run in the prototype 3-litre in 1919. I was quite appalled by the noise; that was my first and most lasting impression. If you glance at the end of this book at the first road test of this car you will see that S. C. H. 'Sammy' Davis of *The Autocar*, who carried out this test, also referred in the kindest terms to this question of noise. The oil pump was the chief culprit, but, while I expected trouble here, I never thought it would make the din that half deafened me on that first trip. We had a form of dry sump lubrication in which the oil was pumped under pressure to the bearings by one pump and a second scavenge pump emptied the oil out of the sump and up into the tank on the dashboard. The gears of those pumps made a quite incredible noise.

Of course, everything made more noise in those days, a fact which is so easy to forget. The reasons for this were the permitted tolerances and the fact that the standard of machining, gear-cutting and general quality of design were all vastly inferior to what we expect today. Also, the actual mountings of the bevel gears, often through ignorance, were not sufficiently rigid, and the result of being off the correct pitch line was a terrible sort of hammering action. Believe it or not, I think that noise is one of the biggest enemies a designer has to fight; and I have spent a good many years in the field of battle, so I should know!

And what about the other things that struck me on that first run? I was pleased with the steering on the whole, and I think the 3-litre always had pleasantly light and precise steering considering the weight of the car and the year of its birth. The suspension, on the other hand, seemed far less satisfactory, and I knew we were going to have to work a lot on that. I was also pleased with the gearbox which never in fact gave serious trouble, and I found the car pleasant to handle through the corners and good on the road. Rather surprisingly, I also found that it was quite tractable in traffic. The brakes, on the other hand, were very noisy, chiefly because we used cast-iron shoes at first, but because of the unusually large drums they were very effective.

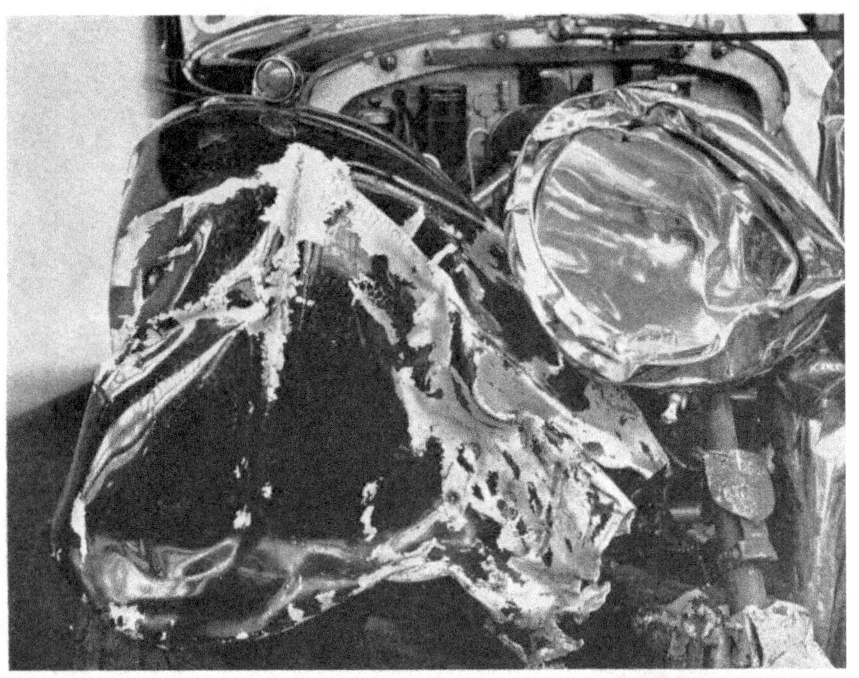

The effect of a Wolseley Hornet on my $3\frac{1}{2}$-litre Rolls-Bentley. The marks of its honeycomb radiator can be seen on the crumpled wing

(*Courtesy British Railways*)

Brush Diesel Electric No. 5503, here hauling the 10.30 a.m.
Liverpool Street–Norwich train

Type 4 2000-h.p. Diesel Electric No. D203 hauling the up
East Anglian Express

(*Courtesy British Railways*)

We subjected that first prototype 3-litre to almost two years of intensive testing, modifying in small ways here and there as required. But during much of this time we were struggling to put arrangements in hand for production of the finished article, which was no easy task at that period when labour and materials were as desperately short as they were later in 1946. It took a judicious blend of hectoring, bullying and patience to complete any sort of production arrangements.

As I have stressed before, we also had to design almost every individual component from universal joints to gearboxes, from back axle to dumbirons; all that I can remember that we were able to obtain from proprietory firms were the Rudge wire wheels, the electrics and the steering wheel. In the end we solved our production problems mainly through a firm at Twickenham which had been on war work and was suddenly, and rather mysteriously, at a complete loss for orders. They did some eighty per cent of the car, while another firm took on the back axle, the gearbox gears and the bevel gears for the engine. By this time—in 1922—we had become not manufacturers of motor cars as we had intended, but assemblers and testers, and that remained our function almost until the end. In fact the only car for which we did any machining ourselves was that curious and little-lamented 4-litre car.

We were also, as we were to learn to our cost later, entirely in the hands of these two firms. We had no alternative means of supply and they appreciated this dilemma only too keenly, charging us stiff prices, which became inflated again if we ordered even the most minute modification.

How easy to be wise after the event! But it was not long before we saw the error of our ways and recognized that we should have held up production or taken substantial deposits from purchasers long before their cars went into production.

We very soon did away with the double oil pump on the 3-litre and went over to a new form of wet sump lubrication in which the oil was carried in a container under the main sump, and free of it so that it was constantly surrounded by cooling air. This was satisfactory but rather expensive and we soon had to drop this, too, converting to orthodox wet sump.

Another modification we made was to convert to two magnetos, which gave us greater power and which were really essential with our two plugs per cylinder. Earlier we had had a single magneto on one side and the water pump on the other.

But the most drastic change we made to the 3-litre was forced on us by the customer, through our sales department. Time and again in those early days we would hear cries of appeal from the sales people who said they could sell twice as many cars if we could only broaden the machine's appeal. 'We had a couple of people in the showrooms this morning,' I would hear, 'and they both liked the car but said there wasn't enough room in the back. And another one wanted a saloon body.'

This sort of complaint brought us nothing but misery for it was the first sign of the car's inevitable perversion. The 3-litre had never been designed to have 'more room in the back'. Above all, it was never designed to carry a saloon body. A closed car demanded a higher standard of silence and this was difficult to attain on a chassis intended originally for open coachwork.

But, as usual, the design department had to yield because I appreciated perfectly well that we had to make changes if we were to continue to stay alive. So we produced, with as good a grace as we could muster, a long-chassis model, and to make life endurable for saloon passengers we fitted a double silencer exhaust system, and went to spiral bevel gears on the camshaft drive.

Of course, all these things were not necessarily retrograde, and certainly by curing the bugbear of piston slap we made a considerable step forward. The early cars all had hour-glass pistons, but eventually only a split-skirt piston was fitted, except to those cars used for racing.

This may have been the first flexible piston ever, and later became known as the B.H.B. (or Bentley Hewitt Burgess) piston. The piston was Burgess's idea and I never believed it would work, but it did, and very well too.

The 3-litre, then, was a car designed for the specific purpose of travelling long distances over indifferent roads at high speeds, with safety, and with the greatest reliability factor we could hope for. In these respects I think it was quite successful. It was a good, fast touring car for long journeys, built at a time when the average moderate-sized machine had a maximum speed of around 50 m.p.h. Its steering, suspension and brakes made it quite safe, and it was more reliable than most of its contemporaries because it could not be overdriven. That it could have been made faster was proved by us and by many enthusiastic Bentley Drivers' Club members who have done things with the car that have made my hair stand on end! I would never have thought it possible after all these years.

Very shortly after the 3-litre went into full production a new market had begun to develop in Britain. The demand for a rugged, open-air, semi-sporting vehicle was soon satisfied, and of course the sales people at Bentley Motors were not being obtuse when they began to complain that many people who admired our cars for their speed and reliability also wanted— if only for the comfort of their wives—something that was a good deal more refined and that could take luxury closed coachwork without sacrificing performance.

A closed body in the 3-litre was always an anachronism, as it only emphasized the noise, although a convertible with a leather top was much quieter. We recognized that the only way we could meet this new demand was by increasing the size of the engine and going to six cylinders. This was inevitable, and I did not regret the birth of the Big Six, which was later to become, as the Speed Six, the most successful sporting car we made, works entries in competition winning nearly every race for which they were entered. I suppose its most publicized win at the time was at Le Mans, the first half of which was the most exciting struggle in our competition history. I have always thought it a pity that Benjafield's account of this race in *The Bentleys at Le Mans* has been out of print for so long, and I have therefore added it to the Appendices at the end of this book. The lap chart alone is worth some close study!

The Six cost very little more to make than the 3-litre, and we could charge very much more for it. Like its successor, the 8-litre, it had a much higher unit rate of profit than the smaller car. There was no question of course at this time or later, as some people have suggested, of our making a bread-and-butter car as we had no production facilities. It would have been even more ridiculous than suggesting that Rolls-Royce or Hispano-Suiza should go into competition with Morris or Citroen. A bread-and-butter car has to be made in huge quantities and we had neither the capital nor the means to do this.

A smaller car was equally out of the question when times became difficult for our excellent sales staff. A small, hand-built or hand-assembled luxury car is almost as expensive as a large one, as you gain only in the reduced weight of metal. Rolls-Royce found this out later with their $2\frac{3}{4}$-litre, 18-h.p. car. R-R of course demanded the same standards of workmanship and finish on this as on their Phantoms, and when the costing people came up with their figures there was great consternation when it was discovered that it was going to be almost as expensive as the 20-25-h.p. car. It was also, incidentally, quite as fast as the larger car, too, as I discovered when I drove it round Brooklands. With the $2\frac{3}{4}$-litre I put up times rather better than I could manage with the 20-25-h.p. to the distress of all present.

Looking back now over the twelve years of life of the Bentley Company, I can see that, perhaps unconsciously, I followed certain principles of policy on the design and engineering side. I don't want to seem to attach too much importance to this, not least because by now far too much has already been written about a small company that ceased to exist thirty years ago. But I can't help feeling that there are certain lessons still to be learnt from our practice of testing relentlessly our cars under the conditions to which they might be subjected during a strenuous life.

I did a great deal of this testing myself, driving a new model many thousands of miles all over the Continent, seeking the worst possible combination of extreme gradients, temperature, and road conditions I could find. Type testing was almost an obsession with me, and I cannot begin to list the snags and failings I ferreted out during these prolonged runs. But I would think nothing of taking my Six up to Carlisle and back between nine in the morning and eleven at night, in order to forestall possible complaints. On these runs, not only did I hope to cure the specific point but discover other things about the car that might be improved. There are numerous things that you find out when you are tired after a really long journey, because under these conditions everything is magnified—faults in the seats, rake of the steering column, or perhaps certain noises and fumes, as well, of course, as any failings in the car's handling. I have always found remarkable (as I suspect have numerous purchasers of new cars) how many faults in a motor are overlooked after only a brief run.

All the time I was with Bentley Motors and Lagondas I succeeded in keeping myself detached from the day-to-day problems of theory and detail. And I do think that this passion of mine for going out on to the road to *drive* and see for myself should be more applied than it is today. For one thing, the stakes are much higher. Tooling up for a new car today involves a capital expenditure probably ten times as high as the total turnover of Bentley Motors from birth to death. Yet I am certain that many new models that have appeared from British manufacturers in the past fifteen years have had the barest minimum of experimental testing, judging by the results, anyway.

Turning now from slight self-commendation to self-criticism,

I must regret that I didn't spend more time driving other cars, especially during the Bentley Motors period. I should have liked to take out at least once a year for a really prolonged test every model that was remotely comparable to ours, but somehow we seemed always to be so hard-pressed for time, and everyone was working at such full pressure, that I never got round to this. But this in no way invalidates my theory that far too many people associated with the design and development of cars, both today and in the past, are so sunk in their own work that they don't bother even to glance out of the windows of their ivory towers.

This is not just a question of seeking out and curing the faults in one's own cars; it is also a matter of finding out what the others are up to. To build a good new motor car you have to be prepared to copy intelligently and draw your ideas from the whole world.

Originality for the sake of originality is not in itself meritorious, and for many years now there has been practically no scope for originality anyway, except possibly in transmissions. Somebody at some time has done almost everything; and even the permutations are becoming exhausted.

As an illustration of this strongly held view of mine it might be helpful to run through in the broadest outline what we did in the car line while I was at Lagondas for some ten years. When I arrived at Staines in 1935 one of the many models in production was the 4½-litre Meadows-engined six-cylinder car, a rough and rugged but quite fast and reliable machine that had just won at Le Mans, to the surprise of everyone, including its entrants.

We re-vamped this six-cylinder very thoroughly, improving the chassis as well as the engine, and giving special attention to valve gear that had been excessively noisy, and the cam profiles. With development the Rapide became quite an acceptable car, and I believe that for a short time it was the fastest catalogued unsupercharged British car. But it was quite evidently an obsolescent design with its long-stroke engine, and was not (nor intended to be) comparable as a fast, luxurious touring carriage to the 8-litre Bentley of nearly a decade earlier.

What we were after above all in this new car was mechanical refinement and silence combined with turbine-like power, particularly in the higher speed range. To achieve this we went straight up to twelve cylinders, believing that this arrangement, among other things, would provide us with the advantage of the highest possible number of impulses per mile, an important factor in a town carriage at low speed. On a big-bore four- or six-cylinder car the torsional impulses are necessarily evident, at low speeds in particular. With twelve cylinders arranged in V-form, we thought we could get the shortest and strongest possible crankshaft combined with the strongest crankcase, and also a four-bearing crankshaft that would provide us with the virtually vibration-free engine at which we were aiming.

A four-bearing crankshaft with an engine of this cubic capacity was considered a bit revolutionary, and so was the very high crankshaft speed. But we worked on the principle that if an engine is vibration-free and there is no noticeable increase in noise, then there is every advantage in a high-revving engine. In fact, the V12 would run happily up to 6000 r.p.m. and was still quiet at this speed, and we achieved our aim of producing a car that, with approximately the same capacity as the 6-cylinder car, if fitted with its gear ratios, would have been as fast in third as the Meadows-engined car was in top. This gave us a very good top-gear performance, which was a prime requirement and, as you will see in Appendix II at the end of this book, was favourably referred to at the time.

In the V12, of course, we used the single overhead camshaft. This time, however, we operated it through a chain drive, which we had earlier decided might be unsatisfactory for the Bentley range. But since then many advances had been made in the chain gear that had caused some overhead camshafts to be so noisy. Chains in any context hate speed; they whip about and generally run riot in a thoroughly disorderly manner. Fast-moving chains can be the very devil. In the V12 we got round this drawback in some degree by running a gear from the crankshaft to a shaft like that used in side-valve engines, and drove the camshaft chains from that, so reducing their speed by half, and making them shorter, quieter and generally more efficient.

However, I do not want to get technically involved in the V12 Lagonda as most people know all about it and probably remember it in detail much better than I do. It is less likely, however, that many people know what happened to the last fifty or so V12 engines, or that they became involved, in an unusual manner, in competition with the Alfa Romeo.

This came about because, shortly after Italy entered the war, Malta harbour was attacked by a squadron of unique and highly dangerous hydroplanes that can best be described as manned torpedoes. We received the first and highly secret information about them at Lagondas when we got an urgent appeal from the Admiralty at Bath saying that they were interested in the V12 engine and could we come down at once for consultations.

Dick Watney, Lagonda's Managing Director at that time, arrived to find the Admiralty in a state of some excitement over a signal recently received from Malta describing this hydroplane attack. It seemed that they were very fast machines each manned by a volunteer who steered his craft with its 5 cwt. of explosive in the nose straight for the harbour shipping from its parent submarine. He was equipped with an ejector seat and a rubber dinghy and he had recourse to these when the hydroplane leapt over the harbour boom at some forty knots.

This feat was accomplished with the assistance of an ingenious arrangement by which the bevel-driven vertical shaft driving two contra-rotating propellers was swivelled out of the water, and back into it again when the obstacle had been passed. The engine, the naval signal related, was by Alfa Romeo, probably a 3-litre twin overhead camshaft one.

The Admiralty thought that the V12, tuned to some 240 b.h.p. and with four carburettors as we had used at Le Mans, was the most suitable engine to power a similar craft to offset this Italian menace, particularly I imagine because of its low weight. Vospers were brought in for the hull, and we were told that the first machines would be expected within three months. This deadline was, in fact, met, although it meant a tremendous pressure of work at Staines and Southampton, and a very tight liaison between us.

Some time after the prototype was finished, the navy succeeded in capturing one of the Italian hydroplanes, which had run up on to the beach in Malta harbour and had failed to explode. The similarity with our own was astonishing, even down to small points of transmission detail, in spite of the fact that neither Vospers nor Lagondas had more than the most uncertain cabled details of the Italian machines.

Peter du Cane of Vospers did a number of highly dangerous trial runs in our boats, and I think they were finally developed as practical weapons of destruction; in fact experiments were also carried out with dropping them (manned by a dummy) from Sunderland flying boats at low level, although whether on impact the engine went through the hull I never discovered. But I don't think they were ever used in combat, and I don't believe the Alfas did any more damage than the Lagondas.

I have included at the end of this book one of the first road tests of the V12 car, which makes interesting reading, even the performance figures standing up to comparison with most big five-seater saloons of today, especially if one remembers that the Lagonda weighed about two tons. I think it is fair to say that the V12 was a good luxury semi-sporting car with quite considerable power, and I am only sorry now that its life was so brief. But it was by no means perfect, even after a year of production. The main trouble was that it was produced in a hurry and under management pressure. It is always the same story: when you are in a hurry, you not only make mistakes, but you make the car too heavy and too complicated. To reach the simplest and therefore the best conclusions always takes time, and to lose weight takes longer still.

The frame of the V12 was too heavy, as was the steering. I think we could have improved the car in these respects if we had had the time and the experimental facilities—not that that excuses these faults in the least, and in fact we had some really excellent men on the experimental side; there just weren't enough of them. Also the power of the V12 was not good low down, where it is most wanted, on British roads anyway. This was because the valve setting favoured the top end. We never even had a chance to absorb the lessons of Le Mans. We took two of the cars there in 1939, with specially prepared four-carburettor engines and lightweight, streamlined bodies. It was a trial run-out for them of course—and against my wishes, too, as I didn't think we were ready for that sort of thing—in which they were set to run at a speed fractionally above that of the winner the previous year. This they did, like clockwork, without ever being pressed, without tyre change or brake adjustment, and the two cars came in quite satisfactorily third and fourth.

After the war I was very keen to drop the V12. I didn't think there would be a market for that kind of car. But how wrong I was! And I take the entire blame for its failure to revive, for the sales people were very keen that we should market it again. By lightening the frame and improving the steering, by modifying the camshafts to produce more power low down, and a few other modifications, we could have had a car to stand without disgrace alongside other high-performance cars in the higher price range, anyway for quite a few years after the war.

Instead we produced the 2½-litre, the last car for which I was responsible, and the only one which had a production run of more than ten years. Although it had a negligible competition record, the same engine, or the same engine in developed form, did well for David Brown in the Aston Martin.

Earlier in this chapter I emphasized my contention that a

good designer must 'draw from the world', searching for the best features or combination of features to incorporate in his own creation. Many a good design has been ignorantly criticized by people who have said: 'Oh, that idea was pinched from the so-and-so,' and 'Of course, he copied this from the other.' This line of argument can be used to 'prove' that every feature of every motor car on the market today was stolen from some previous design.

To underline the point I am trying to make, let's take a look at some of the components of the 2½-litre—at the camshaft-drive chains for example. In spite of their successful application to the earlier V12, we were still not altogether happy about very high speed chains, which so often in the past had caused almost as much noise and disturbance as all the rest of the engine and transmission put together. But the 2½-litre was intended to be a cheaper and simpler car than the V12, and we were tempted to run the chains at a higher speed than on the bigger car for these reasons—and in fact they did not make that amount of noise after the flutter periods were damped out with the damper we developed.

For the V12 car we had used the Weller patent spring strip under licence. Weller, of A.C. cars, had invented many years earlier a hardened steel strip in the rough form of a bow, which pressed against the bed of the chain, steadying it during vibration periods. This had not been altogether satisfactory, as prolonged wear on the plates sometimes caused them to break. So when we were considering the camshaft drive chains for the 2½-litre car after the war, we had to think again, eventually coming up with an idea of our own, using a piston and oil pressure.

During all my years as a designer, I spent much of my time studying technical magazines—and not just contemporary ones either—catalogues, service manuals, and so on. I have always thought it an absolute duty of everyone in the design department to search through printed sources in order to note the successes and failures of others, and the general trends of the time. It was thus, and quite by chance, that I saw the answer to one problem of ours in a pre-war Salmson catalogue. Describing the very advanced British Salmson 14-h.p. engine, it said:

Twin camshafts are situated directly over the inclined valves and operate tappets which take the form of a small piston working in a cylindrical guide. The arrangement imposes all the side thrust on the tappets and none on the valves. The upper end of each tappet is recessed for a tappet plate, the top surface of which is case-hardened while the under-side is hollowed out to receive an aluminium pad which effectively acts as a silencer.

A good drawing further clarified this arrangement, which I thought ingenious and obviously effective, and so likely exactly to fill our need that we at once began experimental work ourselves on the same lines. A similar arrangement was finally adopted and proved wholly satisfactory.

Wet cylinder liners for the Lagonda, with their obvious advantage of prolonging engine-bore life and reducing the cost of overhaul, seemed another good idea. More than ten years earlier Citroen had introduced these, and although few if any other big manufacturers had followed suit, I had thought them admirable in the car I had run; so we used these.

I had also much admired the Citroen's form of rack and pinion steering. This was not a case of imitation because we modified it in numerous ways, including the method of feeding the rack into the pinion in order to reduce back-lash. It was more a case, which is very common in all forms of mechanical engineering design, of using *in principle* a feature which had previously proved its success.

We also utilized a special form of crankshaft mounting. Again, of course, there was nothing really revolutionary in this, and as far as I can remember the arrangement went right back to the Chapuis-Dornier car of around 1910. This was one of the cars for which my brother H.M. and I took over the agency, along with the D.F.P. and several others. Most of them, including the Chapuis-Dornier, were negligible motors and we soon dropped them. But I had been intrigued at the time by the ingenious manner in which the crankshaft was mounted in the crankcase, which was very strong. The crankcase was not split in the usual manner but carried to the bottom, the main bearings being surrounded by aluminium discs of such a size that the crankshaft could pass into the crankcase from the back and the discs were then prevented from revolving. It was good in many ways but I doubt if one would do it again.

Far more commonplace was the source of the con. rod design, from the British Ford in fact. I had been intrigued by the con. rod arrangement in these sturdy bread-and-butter machines before the war, and thought them admirable for our purpose. The top half of the con. rods was formed into prongs instead of separate bolts. What this did do was to make it possible to run a web from the main beam of the rod round the top half of the big end where the head of the big-end bolts are usually located.

The gearbox we made, based on Cotal patents and developed especially by Lagondas, was delightful to use, although it weighed more than an ordinary box.

I could continue this list of source references for some time, but I hope by now that I have established my point. Some designs have owed more to previous practice, others less; the 2½-litre Lagonda can be considered no more than average in the degree of 'imitation' that it contained. In fact, of course, motor-car design is based very largely on an unofficial and unacknowledged free trade agreement, and I have many times noticed with pleasure some of our developed features incorporated in other people's cars!

As I have emphasized earlier, the one great fundamental in engineering design is compromise; and as time goes on and there remain fewer and fewer new things to be discovered about the internal combustion engine, the means of propelling and springing it, and of constructing the framework in which it is placed, this compromise will tend to cause the design teams to become a juggling and balancing act to achieve the best arrangement of components and contrivances for the intended purpose.

The decision whether or not to use a particular component, or arrangement of components, depends on, first its quality, second its suitability for the overall design and third its suitability for meeting any legislation demands. Examples that immediately come to mind drawn from my own experience of only one car are the slow-revving, low-compression, long-stroke 3-litre Bentley: slow-revving because the valve gears and bearings at that time did not like rapid movement; low compression because the petrol was so poor; and the stroke was long because of the current taxation system that was based on bore only. Today, of course, if I were going to produce a 3-litre high-performance car, the dimensions would be quite different, probably over-square so as to make use of all the advantages of a large-bore engine—adequate valves with water between the ports, and so on; the revs could happily go up to twice what the old 3-litre could attain and the compression ratio would be in the order of 8·5 : 1 instead of about 4 : 1.

This one fundamental compromise, which guides the principles of every motor-car designer, taxing his ingenuity and sense of balance, is something we all have to face at some level when we have to build anything, from a garden shed to a week-end sloop. I had a nice example of it recently when I designed for myself and my wife a small house.

I was restricted by the area of land at my disposal, and, by the local authorities, to the square-footage of the structure, and to the roof-span and outer and inner wall units by the firm Cotts, who were building it. From the beginning I was beset by a series of problems which taxed my powers of compromise as severely as any of the cars for which I have been responsible.

A very small guest room, or a reasonably comfortable one? Sacrifice the fitted cupboards in my bedroom (containing bound copies of *The Autocar* since 1896) in order to give a guest space to swing a cat? No use pushing my windows out farther as that would make them illegally close to the boundary fence. Have the kitchen sink closer to the hot-water tank in order to save cooling wastage in the pipes at the expense of less convenient position for the china cupboard?

Just as Alec Issigonis placed his engine laterally in the Mini-Minor to enlarge the living space, we gave ourselves more room by throwing out bay windows. The placing of the radiators, the situation of the 800-gallon oil tank, the opening of every door for the greatest convenience, the height of every cupboard in the kitchen to suit both my wife and myself—every decision on these and a hundred other points was settled by the designer's hated enemy and closest friend—compromise!

Now that I have designed my last engine, my last car and also, I expect, my last house (for that has perhaps been my one real success!) I find that my engineering and design interest has gone a full circle. I am back now with my locomotives, which gave me so much pleasure more than half a century ago. I do not, of course, do any creative work, but I am tremendously interested in everything that goes on.

Locomotives came back into my life like this. When my autobiography was published I received an astonishing number of letters from people all over the world, some of whom I remembered well, and others whose lives had just brushed up against mine at some time. These gave me a great deal of pleasure and reminded me of many half-forgotten incidents— problems shared over the drawing-board, over an engine, over a pit counter. I had not realized before how a book could bring back so many faces from the past.

Other people wrote to me because they had flown or serviced B.R.-engined planes, or owned a D.F.P. or a Bentley or had seen our cars win at Le Mans or Brooklands; there were all sorts of reasons, and they were all nice letters to receive. Among these correspondents was a man called Richard Hardy, who is today only thirty-seven but had served part of his apprenticeship at Doncaster under the same foreman as I had thirty or more years before.

Hardy is now on the locomotive side of the Eastern Region of British Railways, and after the exchange of several letters he came along to our house to see me one day. We talked a great deal about the railways as I knew them at the beginning of the century, about our respective apprenticeships, and about the railways today. Before he left he suggested that I should take some rides on the footplate of some Eastern Region locomotives.

Of course, I jumped at the chance. It had been a long time since I had held a footplate pass, which is one of the most privileged and difficult-to-secure tickets in the country. There then followed a number of very interesting trips out of Liverpool Street, some on diesel-electric locomotives and others on steam locos, to Ipswich and Colchester.

Several things in particular impressed me about these journeys, mostly favourable. First and most important was the tremendously high state of morale of all those whom I met at Liverpool Street and Stratford. This applied not only to the supervisory staff but also particularly to the footplate men—the late Inspector Wally Mason, drivers like A. E. Fairbrother, R. Nichols, A. Wickens of Stratford, Stan Pittock of Clacton and Bob Baker of Enfield. To meet these men, and many like them on all regions of British Railways, highly skilled, loyal, devoted to their calling, a grand bunch of men, is one of the most reassuring and pleasant things you can do today. It is also the best answer to give anyone who says that trade unionism and the welfare state have finished off the traditional qualities of the British.

One day a few months ago I was taken on the footplate out of Liverpool Street on a rush-hour suburban steam train. This was an experience I will not forget for a long time, and as an exercise in human skill in overcoming the handicaps of obsolete machinery under difficult conditions it would be hard to match anywhere. The driver was an Enfield man, Bob Baker, who started on the L.N.E.R. at King's Cross, and the fireman a

(*Courtesy British Railways*)

The Bristolian at Mill Lane

Eastern Region N.7/5 class o—6—2T at Stratford

(*Courtesy R. E. Vincent*)

(*Courtesy British Railways*)

English Electric 'Deltic' 3300-h.p. Diesel Electric locomotive
at Doncaster

Standard 7MT Pacific 'Hereward the Wake' at Cambridge

(*Courtesy R. E. Vincent*)

young man by the name of Harding. The locomotive, Baker's regular engine, was a long-travel valve N.7 class, No. 9719, a small suburban tank engine now withdrawn from service, drawing an absolutely packed train-load of commuters, and had to halt at countless suburban stations, to be precise thirteen stations in eleven miles. The rails were greasy, the ten-coach train scarcely fitted some of the shorter platforms and the timing was a tight one. And yet, by dextrous manipulation of the regulator valve gear and the Westinghouse brake together with most careful firing to avoid wasting steam, driver and fireman co-operated to exercise an old skill that uniquely combines a test of delicate timing and great strength, so that wheelslip was avoided in spite of the great weight, the train was brought to a swift but steady halt on the mark at every platform, and the schedule was maintained almost to the second.

It was a triumph; there is no other word for it. And yet, under the most difficult conditions, this was an operation that was carried out daily by these two men (prior to the very recent electrification) and by many more who operate these old suburban locomotives in and out of our big cities every night and morning, summer and winter. I take my hat off to them.

On several occasions I asked these drivers what they thought about the new diesel and electric age looming up ahead of them, and whether they preferred to be in the cab of say a Brush Diesel-Electric or on the footplate of a Britannia. I always found them reluctant to commit themselves, and I could see the conflict between old loyalties and affection for the traditional romance of steam and the cleanliness, convenience and comparative simplicity of the new way. It wasn't really a fair question to ask. But during my travels I met two men who particularly impressed me because of the way they accepted the new order and were determined to educate themselves in diesel lore at every available opportunity. I was taken to the new Stratford diesel depot by a young man called Thorn. He was about thirty-eight, had served his apprenticeship on steam in the running shed at Stratford during the rough war years, and worked in Stratford and Southend Sheds as a fitter until 1956, when he became a shed master. In 1958 he was selected for special diesel training and since then has devoted his life to a study of diesel traction. We spent a couple of hours in the engine room of a Brush locomotive discussing technicalities and I was amazed that a practical steam man could absorb so quickly and thoroughly an entirely new and different branch of mechanical and electrical engineering.

On the Western Region the same thing applied. When I travelled out of Paddington on the Bristolian, I was accompanied by Inspector W. Andress. He was now a locomotive inspector, stationed at Paddington, but specializing in diesel traction. His thirty-five years of railway work had been solely devoted to steam, first as a cleaner, then as a fireman, then as a driver and ultimately as an inspector. Here he was, at middle age, changing his outlook, and changing it completely and successfully, with tremendous enthusiasm.

A memorable journey on a large Deltic—opposed piston, three-crankshaft Napier diesel-electric engine—from Doncaster to King's Cross after a visit to my old works at Doncaster— showed me all too clearly how quickly the old age of steam is passing by. This changeover period is difficult for many men. There are many reasons for this. Steam took a tremendous pasting during the last war. Maintenance went down to a low ebb, conditions in running sheds deteriorated and after the war, with the general change in working conditions and hours of employment in industry throughout the country, together with the existence of full employment, steam locomotive running and maintenance lost much of its former attraction. Railway wages were not high and men left the job in thousands during the 1950s. Thus the steam locomotive tended to become neglected at depots where the shortages were greatest. With the advent of the diesel and the start of the modernization programme new maintenance depots were built, incorporating amenities such as were never dreamt of by past generations of railwaymen.

Standards of cleanliness, and conditions generally, have started to improve again, and in many places this has already had its effect and men are coming back to the railways.

The French were lucky. Their lines were so thoroughly destroyed that they were forced to start from scratch again in 1946, and they not only have thousands of miles of the most excellent permanent way, but employ some of the most advanced techniques in electric and diesel traction in Europe.

But British Railways were forced to pick at the problem, and until recently they've never had the money to do more than patch here and there. The consequence is that many main lines in Britain have, from time to time in the past fifteen years, been bedevilled by repair work and consequent speed restrictions. Now this does not mean only hard work and frustration for the drivers and firemen, who just get things running nicely when they have to shut off again for another speed order. With a steam locomotive this is also a pretty uneconomic business. There is nothing a steam locomotive hates more than frequent stopping and starting. Remembering the frustration and fury that I felt as a fireman at the very rare unscheduled stops we had in the old days, I don't know how the footplate men have stood it for so long! But on a diesel, of course, a check is scarcely more trouble to the driver than a red traffic light to a motorist. He just applies his brake, comes down to the speed prescribed, blows his brake off, opens the throttle, and the diesel traction motors and 2000 h.p. do the rest.

We all thought a short time ago, when the giant modernization plan for the railways was announced, that this patching-up of locomotives, track, culverts and bridges, tunnels and so on, would be done away with. Tremendous strides were made but the latest news once again is that the Government is going to trim down the modernization programme after all. This sort of thing has been going on for so long, with unpredictable switches, that the enthusiasm and goodwill of the railwaymen has been stretched almost to breaking point. It makes one despair of democratic government, and sometimes, too, of the policy of putting civil servants into the top positions. Very few railways can pay their way under the economic conditions in many countries today. But if the taxpayer has got to underwrite the cost, as he does in Germany, France and Italy, let us do it sensibly and honestly with proper long-term planning that can't be fiddled about by Whitehall, and with a thought for the fact that railways are run by men—good men.

Having taken me to Doncaster Works and on the Deltic from Doncaster to King's Cross, Mr T. C. B. Miller, the Chief Mechanical and Electrical Engineer of the Eastern Region, arranged for me to travel on the footplate of the diesel loco-motive working the Bristolian from Paddington to Bristol. I do not suppose that many people have enjoyed the pleasure and excitement of riding in the driving cab of a modern diesel locomotive. It is an experience not easily forgotten.

The Bristolian is tightly timed but the schedule could be easily maintained by the Swindon built machine on which I travelled.

This locomotive was one of the Maybach-engined Diesel-hydraulics, a form of diesel traction to which I am drawn, because, I suppose, I am slightly suspicious of the added compli-cations that the diesel electric involves. The Maybach engine is made under licence in this country by Bristol-Siddeley and is a V12 developing 1100 b.h.p. at 1530 r.p.m. Transmission is through a four-speed box, with a torque convertor working between the automatic changes; curiously enough, the same type of gearbox was on the twelve-cylinder Maybach car in which I was once driven by young Maybach, the son of the firm's founder. The Bristolian's locomotive had two of these engines, forward and aft, separated by compartments for heating the train and cooling the oil and water.

The first thing that impressed me when I arrived at Paddington for this trip was that the diesel had just arrived from Plymouth, and that, without any sort of maintenance, it was going to run to Bristol and back, and then back to Ply-mouth before any attention was paid to it. I was also told that she did one mile to the gallon, which seemed astonishingly good for two motors developing well over 2000 h.p.

As I went into the forward cab, and noted the cleanliness, and comfort, my mind went back to the old G.N. Atlantics on which I used to work. On these you were fortunate if you got a chance to sit on the bit of wood that formed the fireman's seat, which folded down against the left-hand side of the cab. I glanced at the many gauges and indicators, and at the throttle handle, and remembered the simple regulator and reversing lever of the Atlantic, the light and handy firing shovel and the cloth one always had to use on an Atlantic to avoid burning one's left hand on the shovel blade. Then I noted the admirable little electric cooking stove for the use of the enginemen—and remembered those lamb chops we used to grill on the shovel over a low fire before making up the fire again to start our journey home. How good they tasted! Plush seats, ashtrays, drinking water to hand, built-in demisters, windscreen wipers. What a contrast! And an excellent thing, too.

The next thing that struck me as we moved steadily and almost silently out of Paddington was the remarkable visibility and the wonderful driving position. There was no longer any question of leaning out and peering forward through a small window. Here we were, sitting high up and with glass all round. It was better than the observation car on a Canadian train crossing the Rockies.

This driving position also took a little getting used to. I felt distinctly uneasy at first, with no protective thirty-feet-or-so of boiler in front, and the rails seemed to come whipping up to meet you at an alarming rate. Splendid but vulnerable! The sense of power as we thrust forward along Brunel's old line, with 350 tons of train behind us and those great diesels beating out a steady rhythm, was most impressive. After I got over my nervousness, I found myself half hypnotized by the track racing beneath, and to watch the radius of a long curve arching ahead and then flashing towards you was something I'll never forget.

We did the last part of the return journey in the dark, and

that was tremendously impressive, too. But I will not risk boring you with any more lyrical descriptions. For many British Railways drivers this is a commonplace experience, although to someone brought up on steam over fifty years ago it was an interesting and exciting experience.

The charm and wonder of the locomotive was deeply instilled in me as a boy, and if only I were thirty years younger I should not hesitate to surrender myself to their power and fascination again. I am certain that I should find the life as compelling as I did fifty years ago when I left it for the hurly-burly of the motor industry.

Appendix One

This account of our last race at Le Mans was written by the late Dr J. B. Benjafield some fourteen years ago and remains the best that I know of our tussle with the Mercedes.

LE MANS 1930

Early in 1930 I received an invitation to drive for the supercharged team for the whole of the coming season, which I accepted without hesitation.

This is no place to describe the troubles and tribulations of those endeavouring to prepare a team of cars for a season's racing, with less than half the minimum of time normally necessary for such a project available. Anyway such was the position, and many were the nights that the 'Brains' of the side went short of sleep. In their optimism, three of the S/C 4½s were entered for Le Mans and, miracle of miracles, three cars left the Welwyn Works under their own steam, bound for Le Mans a week before the race. To say that they were ready for the race would be a gross exaggeration, and the amount of work done by the very able and interested mechanics during that last week was incredible. The drivers for the three cars were as follows: Car No. 1 Tim Birkin and Jean Chassagne; Car No. 2 Ramponi and Dr J. D. Benjafield; and Car No. 3 George Eyston and Beris Harcourt Wood.

To add to our difficulties, we found that the fuel allowed by the regulations caused our engines to overheat, and in order to overcome this trouble it was decided on the Thursday afternoon (48 hours before the race) that all the supercharged team should run on pure Benzol, which oddly enough was permissible, although a petrol-benzol mixture which would suit the engine was not allowed. Anyway, in order to get the best out of this fuel, it was necessary to raise the compression of the engines. To accomplish this, a plate had to be removed from beneath the cylinder block and it was only possible to complete this alteration on two of the cars in time for the race, and so only cars No. 1 and 2 came under the starter's orders. It was awfully bad luck for George and Beris, but there was nothing we could do about it and it was only through the courtesy and helpfulness of the Leon-Bollee works at Le Mans that cars Nos. 1 and 2 were ready in time. It was by no means the first occasion on which this firm had come to our rescue in a crisis of this kind, and on behalf of the Bentley teams that have driven at Le Mans I would like to take this opportunity of thanking them.

By contrast, the official Bentley Motors Ltd. team of three 6½-litre was a haven of peace. The three cars were beautifully turned out, and split-pinned down to the last possible nut. They did indeed appear a worthy team of cars to uphold the good name of the country that had produced them. The drivers of the work's team were: Car No. 1 Captain Woolf Barnato (twice winner) and Lieut.-Commander Glen Kidston; Car No. 2 Frank Clement and Dick Watney; and Car No. 3 Sammy Davis and Clive Dunfee. By the way, the numbers used in describing the drivers of the two teams bear no relation to the numbers allotted to the cars in the race.

The works team and the supercharged team were quite separate, the pits of the former being managed by Mr Clarke and those of the latter were in the able hands of Kensington Moir. And thus of the three Speed-Sixes and three S/C 4½-litres which had crossed the Channel a week earlier, five only were ready to face the starter at 4 p.m. on June 21st 1930. It was the first time we had failed to get all our cars on to the starting-line, though as a matter of fact the supercharged cars were hardly out of the experimental stage.

The mere fact that two of the supercharged cars were ready in time, in my opinion, reflected great credit on all those responsible for having accomplished so much in so little time, for it was not until the preceding autumn that a definite start had been made.

The entry for this year's race was a small one, totalling only nineteen cars, but what it lacked in quantity it certainly made up for in quality, as may be judged from the following list:

Car No.		Drivers
1.	Supercharged Mercedes	Caracciola and Werner
2.	6½-litre Bentley	Clement and Watney
3.	6½-litre Bentley	Davis and Clive Dunfee
4.	6½-litre Bentley	Barnato and Kidston
5.	Stutz	Phillipe and Bouriat
6.	Stutz	Brisson and Rigal
7.	4½-litre Bentley s/c (non-starter)	Eyston and Harcourt-Wood
8.	4½-litre Bentley s/c	Ramponi and Benjafield
9.	4½-litre Bentley s/c	Birkin and Chassagne
10.	Alfa-Romeo	Howe and Callingham
11.	Talbot	Lewis and Eaton
12.	Talbot	Hindmarsh and Rose-Richards
13.	2-litre B.N.C.	
14.	Lea-Francis	Peacock and Newsome
15.	Bugatti	Mesdames Mareuse and Siko
16.	Tracta	Gregoire and Vallon
17.	Tracta	Bourcier and Debeugny
18.	M.G. Midget	Samuelson and Kindell
19.	M.G. Midget	Murton and Neale

The withdrawal of No. 7 Eyston and Harcourt-Wood's S/C 4½-Bentley, left eighteen cars to face the starter on the Saturday afternoon at 4 o'clock. It promised to be one of the most exciting and toughly contested sports-car races ever held, for in spite of the invincible reputation Bentleys had gained in this particular race, the entry, small as it was, had a very definite international flavour. Germany, America, Italy, France and Great Britain were all represented, and any one of the first twelve might be in the lead after twenty-four hours' running, for the speed in the opening stages of the race was sure to be a hot one, resulting in a high casualty list especially heavy amongst the fastest cars. Who would be bold enough to rule out the possibility of the race being won by one of the new Talbots? The S/C Mercedes had a great reputation for speed and was being handled by very skilled and experienced drivers. As regards numbers, Bentleys had an enormous advantage and it was long odds in favour of at least one of the five finishing, with little or no trouble, which would mean a pretty high average speed. On the other hand, if the 'Merc' could stay the course, he was going to take a lot of catching.

At a luncheon given on the Wednesday before the race, at which the Mercedes personnel and the official Bentley Motors Ltd. team were guests, and into which by some mistake I managed to insinuate myself, there were enough lies told to sink a battleship. Each side outvied the other in the speeds they had clocked for the circuit, and the speed at which they got through any given bend, speeds which, as long as the laws of gravity obtained, must land one in the ditch. Perhaps this was the idea behind the slight exaggerations, but I prefer to think that it was more the effect of insidious, but none the less pleasant, alcoholism. That very beautiful and charming lady, the late Frau Caracciola, was with her husband and together with her long-haired daschund, 'Fritz', entertained us most delightfully, so much so that there seemed to be some risk that this spirit of friendship might extend to the circuit and neutralize the spirit of competition. In fact, I pretended to deplore the whole thing and accused Sammy Davis and Dick Watney of 'fraternizing' with the enemy. I have quite forgotten who was responsible for this luncheon party which was successful in bringing together the chief members of the two most important teams running, but it was an excellent idea, and one that might be repeated with advantage.

At long last the great day dawns; Saturday, June 21st, and it looks like being a scorcher; better that than wet, though a cloudless sky in the late afternoon makes the run down to Arnage pure hell, as it is here that the direction of the road is due west and the last two hours before sunset the light is very trying.

Shortly after three o'clock the cars are lined up in front of the pits in a staggered row, the engines are run for a few minutes to warm them up, switched off and the hard racing plugs are substituted for the softer road ones and once more the engine is started to make sure that all the news plugs are firing, and after two or three bursts up to two-five she is once more switched off and covered up with an old rug. With fifteen minutes to go, Babe Barnato (for the second year in succession) and Tim Birkin, last year's winners, with a couple of marshals in the back with a large yellow flag, set off round the circuit on 'The Lap of Honour', to declare it closed to the public and open for racing. And now with five minutes to go everyone except the opening drivers are herded off the road by the officials. Glen Kidston, Frank Clement and Sammy Davis are opening with the Sixes, whilst Tim Birkin and Ramponi are opening with the Hon. Dorothy Paget S/C 4½-litres. Caracciola is starting with the Mercedes and as the largest car in the race has pride of place at the head of the line. At flag-fall he takes full advantage of this position and the long, low, white car streaks away with the supercharger screaming, closely followed by Kidston and Davis, and then a pack of cars which included Tim Birkin with No. 9 and Ramponi with No. 8. Only one car is left on the line, the six-cylinder B.N.C., which had been pushed into its place in feverish haste a few minutes before the start and which, now that the flag had dropped, refused to respond, and had to be pushed off the stage, in dire disgrace, while the Grand Prix d'Endurance is yet only five minutes old.

Owing to the narrow road to Pontlieu and the two bends on the Rue de Circuit, little passing can be done until they come to the Hunaudieres stretch, but once this broad straight stretch is reached No. 9 Bentley goes through the mob like a knife through cheese, so that by the time Mulsanne is reached, the Mercedes is still in the lead, but Glen and Tim are on his tail. Immediately after the bend Birkin forges ahead of Kidston, so that when they come into view of the expectant crowds in the grandstands the low-built, white Mercedes, with its supercharger whining shrilly, is well in the lead, Birkin and Kidston following in close formation, Davis somewhat detached but well within striking distance, ready and anxious to take up the running, should anything go wrong with the leaders. Further reserves are close at hand as both Clement and Ramponi are only a few lengths astern. It is indeed an unequal battle, at any rate as far as numbers are concerned, but whatever the Mercedes firm may have lacked in quantity, they made up for in quality, both as regards machine and drivers. To appreciate the finer points of the really first-class driver, is almost impossible as a mere spectator, however well placed, and in my opinion this can only be achieved by driving in the same race so that he may be kept under observation for a considerable distance. For instance, suppose one is lucky enough to have a seat in the grandstand, what does one see?—merely car after car roaring past on full throttle whether he be a 750-c.c. M.G. or a 6500-c.c. Speed-Six Bentley. Certainly one would have to be built of stone not to be thrilled by the sight of Tim Birkin sitting bolt upright in the S/C 4½ roaring by at 120 m.p.h. at what appears to be about six inches astern of the long low white Mercedes, the shrill whine of whose super-charger monopolizes the sound waves. But as a mere spectator, one misses that superlative artistry possessed by few drivers, and by none in greater degree than Caracciola, that enables him to pass another car on a fast left-hand bend on a wet road with anti-camber. I actually saw him do this in the Tourist Trophy race, the year he won it, as he had passed me shortly before.

At any rate this race promises to provide ample entertainment for the mere spectator, for Ramponi's tail is just disappearing at the beginning of his second lap, when the two black Stutz driven by Philippe (de Rothschild) and Brisson, closely followed by Lord Howe's Alfa and the two Talbots, pass in his wake. Somewhat farther astern is a third group composed of a Bugatti with its feminine crew, a couple of M.G. Midgets and the little Tractas.

Whatever may happen in this Grand Prix d'Endurance de Vingt-Quatre Heures, one thing is certain, and that is that the Bentley-Mercedes duel alone should provide more than sufficient interest to amply repay spectators for coming. At long last could be settled the argument between the protagonists of each marque, as to which was the better and faster car.

Admittedly the numbers five to one seemed a bit unfair, and we had hoped that Mercedes would have sent a team of at least two or, better, three cars to represent them. The fact that they did not send more than one car suggests that one Mercedes would have sufficient speed in hand over any number of Bentleys, to make the result a certainty. Had the Bentleys of 1930 no more speed than that shown in previous years at Le Mans, Mercedes supposition would have been correct, but had they studied the figures of 1924, 1927, 1928 and 1929 with just a little imagination, they should have realized that W.O. does not stand still and that each year that the race was won by Bentley Motors Ltd., the average speed for the race showed a significant increase. That this supposition is correct I have not the slightest doubt, for nothing was farther from the

Mercedes policy than to take a hiding from another nation's car, however great the odds might be. And it was a hiding that he got, fair and square; he was beaten by a better car and were the race run again as a match just between the two cars driven by Barnato and Caracciola, I have no doubt whatever which would prove the victor. It was no fluke, neither did the numbers provide anything more than a tactical advantage. Babe Barnato had sufficient speed to compel Caracciola to use his blower too much in order to keep up with him, and once this fact was established it was only a matter of time before the Merc 'blew up'.

Caracciola's second lap was completed at 86·48 m.p.h., and Tim Birkin who is now forging ahead of Kidston is chasing him, clocking just under 87 m.p.h. for his second lap and 88 m.p.h. for his third. On his fourth lap Birkin catches the Merc and passes him just before Mulsanne, putting his offside wheels well over the grass verge at a speed of little short of 130 m.p.h. to do so. Caracciola had the shock of his life, never dreaming that anything could overtake him. Unfortunately, Tim's car chose this most unsuitable moment to throw a tread from his off-side rear tyre, but he has taken the lead and judging from the speed of his next lap, 6 minutes 48 seconds (89·69 m.p.h.), he intends to keep it. Only by keeping his supercharger in action the whole time can Caracciola keep up. On his sixth lap the fabric of Tim's offside rear tyre bursts, compelling him to reduce speed to 40 m.p.h. The time lost by completing the lap at this speed and changing the wheel at the pit drops Tim back to seventh place, behind all the other Bentleys and Brisson's Stutz.

At the end of the first hour Caracciola is in the lead having covered exactly 85 miles, Sammy Davis and Glen Kidston who are lying second and third are three minutes behind, Ramponi with one of the Dorothy Paget S/C 4½-litres is fourth, Clement fifth, Brisson sixth and Birkin seventh. The two new Talbots driven by Lewis and Eaton, Hindmarsh and Rose-Richards are running very regularly, quiet and fast, and now occupying the eighth and ninth places. Then come the small fry, all of whom are still running and all of whom, with one notable exception, are showing the greatest consideration for their big brothers, keeping well out of their way to facilitate their passing.

At two hours, the leaders are unchanged, but one very significant fact emerges—the gap between the Mercedes and the Davis and Kidston Bentleys has been reduced from three to two minutes, and this in spite of plenty of supercharger. This indeed augured well for the marque Bentley and never before had I seen a smile on the face of the 'Tiger' (W.O.) thus early in the race.

At 6.30 p.m., two and a half hours after the start, the regular fuel stops commence, the first of our lot to come in being Davis with No. 3 Bentley, who was lying second. He and Clive Dunfee do an excellent refill, the 'Plombeurs' affixing the official seals to fuel, oil and water-filler caps in 1 minute 40 seconds. It is only as Clive drives off with No. 3 that Sammy reports that five laps earlier his goggles of 'Splinterless glass' had been hit by a stone thrown up by another car, forcing particles into his left eye. In a flash he substitutes his spare goggles and carries on in spite of great pain without loss of time. Unfortunately all the good work done by Sammy served no good purpose, for this was the last we were to see of No. 3 Bentley. Running down the gradient towards the new Pontlieu curve, about two kilometres after leaving the pits, Clive Dunfee, having passed a Stutz, underestimates his speed, forgets the escape road and tries to take the bend: result—a sickening slither into the sandbank, where the car comes to rest, half-buried. Much frenzied digging by Clive, ably helped by the very disappointed Sammy, using the spare head-light glass merely served to expose a bent front anxle and two buckled wheels. For the team to lose its leading car in this manner is a bitter blow, but fortunately one that it can survive, thanks to the reserves being in close attendance.

The next car in is Ramponi with No. 8. He does the same work in longer time and hands the car over to Dr Benjafield. And now an accident is avoided by the narrowest of margins, an accident that might have caused international complications. Just as No. 8 is gathering speed, Caracciola with the Merc. roars by at somewhere near the 120 m.p.h. mark. Ha, thinks Benjafield, now for a right royal dust-up; let's see if we cannot give the German something to stimulate him, and with this object in mind Benjafield jams the throttle even harder down. At last we're holding him and now, wonder of wonders, we are shortening the gap, and only when the gap between the two cars has shortened to a few yards does Benjafield realize the reason. Caracciola is slowing for the bend, the new bend which cuts out the run down to the village of Pontlieu. So many times has Benjafield driven on the old circuit that in the excitement of the chase he has forgotten the new bend, a kilometre or more short of the old hairpin, and thus he finds himself rushing downhill at an alarming rate, charging straight into the rear of the Mercedes. The road is far too narrow to attempt to pass, especially as the Mercedes is in the middle of the road, never dreaming that anyone would be mad enough to try and pass him in this position. By dint of standing on the brakes and engaging a lower gear at the earliest possible moment the Bentley was just got under control in time; in time to prevent its front springs boring a couple of nasty jagged holes in the petrol tank of the Merc. By the time the Bentley was got under control, there was hardly room for a cigarette paper between the two cars. It requires little imagination to realize what would have been said, and thought, had this accident not been avoided. Anyway that narrow escape plus the sight of No. 3 buried in the sandbank served to bring Benjafield to his senses, and behave with more decorum.

Different drivers, different temperaments, but on the whole, in a long race, a race of this kind, it is safer to go easy for a lap or two—play oneself in so to speak. Twenty-four hours is a long time and it is only on the rarest occasion that the few extra seconds lost by doing this would affect the result.

Glen Kidston with No. 4 is the next car in. In addition to the refuelling a wheel has to be changed so that the total stop takes 3 minutes 18 seconds. No sooner is Barnato away with No. 4 than Clement arrives with the other surviving Speed-Six, No. 2, and it remains for him to show us just how a refill should be done. Every movement is a purposeful one, so much so that he almost appears to be unhurried. His fingers are at the petrol filler cap as the plombeur cuts the seals—in goes the enormous funnel followed by the upturned petrol cans, which are no sooner emptied than they are replaced by full ones and as the cascade of empty petrol cans showering into the pit ceases, he is already tipping in the oil and as soon as oil appears at the overflow tap so is he pouring water into the radiator—this finished and a quick run round the car snapping the spring caps to and as the last seal is being fixed Clement leaps over the pit counter and Dick Watney is engaging first. Pretty to watch, all in 95 seconds—1 minute 35 seconds. It seems incredible, but so important is it to save every possible moment in the pit work when one takes into account the effort expended to save or gain every possible moment in the driving. Five seconds lost in pit work is just as long as five seconds lost in the driving. Clement is an old hand more experienced than any of us and it is once more an example of the difference between the good amateur and the first-class professional. Caracciola is the last to come in and, thanks to rather inferior pit work, the gap between No. 4, now driven by Babe Barnato, which is lying second since the demise of No. 3, is reduced markedly.

For the first time since the Bentleys appeared at Le Mans, they encounter serious tyre trouble. Year after year have they run for the whole 24 hours on one set of tyres, occasionally, perhaps, changing a wheel as a precautionary measure, but this year the supercharged cars, especially, are throwing treads all over the place. Norman Freeman ('Mr Dunlop') is consulted, but fails to explain. The tyres used by the Mercedes, the Speed-Sixes, and the blown cars are the same, yet the two former are enjoying their usual immunity. No, there is nothing wrong with the tyres. The explanation must be sought elsewhere. Actually it was due to a combination of circumstances of which the more important were the heat (it was a very hot afternoon), the weight of the car (47 cwt.) and the rather high centre of gravity plus the high speed of the cars. Whatever the explanation there was no doubt about the fact, of which I had a sharp reminder, approaching Mulsanne on my fourth lap, for the tread of my offside hind wheel parted company with the canvas when the car was doing 120 m.p.h. It made a report like a gunshot, boring a large hole in the wing and shooting up in the air to some prodigious height so that it appeared to be about the size of a blackbird. For the moment I thought some other car had hit me, but as soon as I realized the truth reduced speed till the pits were reached and changed the wheel.

There is a considerable tension in the air—the Mercedes is still in the lead and is setting a cracking pace, but there are two Bentleys in close attendance, No. 4 having taken the place of Davis's car. The blown cars have lost time through the constantly recurring tyre trouble, but in spite of this at the end of the third hour Bentleys hold the second, third and fourth positions, two of the Stutz cars having insinuated themselves ahead of Birkin's car. These American cars have been putting up a most impressive performance. They are non-supercharged straight eights with a special head carrying two camshafts and having four inclined valves per cylinder. They are certainly not as fast as the Bentleys, but Brisson has shown what can be accomplished by steady driving in a race of this kind, for he has succeeded in bringing his car within two minutes of Clement's Bentley after three hours' running. However, all the good work done by Brisson is thrown away for Louis Rigal, who now takes charge of the car, runs off the road on his first circuit, ripping away the exhaust pipe, which has to be secured with wire. Again he gets going and, failing to learn his lesson, again he leaves the road doing still further damage to the underslung exhaust pipe. Result —driving fast past the Café de l'Hippodrome, flames shooting out from the shortened exhaust cause the car to catch fire and the fire gets well established before the driver becomes aware of the fact. However, as soon as he realizes the position, he stands on the brakes, switches off the ignition, grabs the Pyrene and prepares to leap to the road whilst the car is still in motion. His foot, however, gets caught by the top of the door with the result that instead of jumping clear he trips and falls into the middle of the road. It seems impossible that Barnato roaring down the straight on full throttle can miss him, but swerving to one side he accomplishes a miracle and so a tragedy is averted. To add to the drama, the Stutz tank chooses this precise moment to explode, the flames and smoke rising to such a height that they can be seen at Le Mans, five miles away. And thus are the chances of this fine car thrown away.

Caracciola is the last to come in for refuelling—so far he has enjoyed a trouble-free run and has held the lead since the fall of the flag with the exception of Tim's short-lived lead. The pit work here is obviously ill-organized, and many valuable seconds are lost through insufficient rehearsal, seconds which have only been gained at the expense of the supercharger and can ill be spared.

It is at this stage of the race, with Birkin falling back through repeated tyre trouble, No. 3 having been collected by a sandbank, that Capt. Woolf Barnato decides to take up the running and go for the Merc. Anyway, this is the way that we drivers like to think it is, whereas in fact it is the 'Great Man', the *Chef d'Equipe*, or in plain English just W.O., who gives the instructions, playing his pieces like the Master playing chess. By dint of hard driving, shortly before 8.30 p.m., Babe has got on the Merc's tail, and precisely at 8.26 p.m. the Big Six, carrying the number 4, amid vociferous cheers from the British contingent, came roaring past the pits some 50 yards ahead of his German rival. On the next lap, however, by superb driving, Werner, who has taken over from Caracciola, is again in the lead with Barnato 100 yards astern.

This, however, does not disturb the Chief in the least, for it has only been achieved at a price, and a very high price too. We know from past experience that there is one certain way of blowing up a Merc engine and that is by too much use of the supercharger, and Babe is pushing him hard enough, so hard that to keep ahead it means blower most of the time. And now begins that historical Bentley-Mercedes duel, or better, that Barnato-Caracciola duel. A duel between two of the world's finest and fastest production sports-cars driven in each case by the most highly skilled and experienced men England and Germany could produce. Here was a test, a really fair test, under ideal conditions, the result of which would prove, once and for all, which was the better car. Furthermore, here was a test for all the world to see and read about in their papers the following day, a test that would be recorded in black and white in the daily press on the following day and better still in the motor journals in their weekly issues, where it would remain and be available for the enthusiast for all time. Thrilling thought, here was history in the making. So important is the result of this duel, affecting the prestige of the winning car for several years to come, that I propose to give you an extract from the chart kept by Bentley Motors Ltd. in so far as it related to the two cars concerned. I have to thank W.O. for giving me access to these figures (see opposite).

We drivers are getting rather tired of the wreck of No. 5 Stutz, the rear wheels of which are well out into the road, leaving only half the highway free, especially as it is still smouldering and this piece of the circuit is normally quite the fastest and where we big fellows count on being able to pass some of the smaller fry in complete comfort. At last, thank goodness, the officials are doing something about it—high time too, for in another twenty minutes it will be dark. They are connecting a tow-rope to the front of the

COMPARISON OF MERCEDES AND WINNING BENTLEY
LE MANS 1930

Lap	Time — Mercedes hr. min. sec.			Time — Bentley hr. min. sec.			Lead min. sec.		Leading car	Remarks
1		07	23		07	42	0	19	Mercedes	Driver of No. 4 Bentley Com. Glen Kidston, R.N.
2		14	24		15	04	0	40	,,	,, ,, ,, ,,
3		21	22		22	29	1	07	,,	,, , ,, ,,
4		28	22		30	01	1	39	,,	,, ,, ,, ,,
5		35	28		37	21	1	53	,,	,, ,, ,, ,,
6		42	43		44	48	2	05	,,	,, ,, ,, ,,
7		50	02		52	09	2	07	,,	,, ,, ,, ,,
8		57	20		59	30	2	10	,,	,, ,, ,, ,,
9	1	04	38	1	06	44	2	06	,,	,, ,, ,, ,,
10	1	11	56	1	14	06	2	10	,,	,, ,, ,, ,,
11	1	19	13	1	21	16	2	03	,,	,, ,, ,, ,,
12	1	26	29	1	28	30	2	01	,,	,, ,, ,, ,,
13	1	33	46	1	35	52	2	06	,,	,, ,, ,, ,,
14	1	41	04	1	43	06	2	02	,,	,, ,, ,, ,,
15	1	48	18	1	50	42	2	24	,,	,, ,, ,, ,,
16	1	55	36	1	58	02	2	26	,,	,, ,, ,, ,,
17	2	03	00	2	05	18	2	18	,,	,, ,, ,, ,,
18	2	10	15	2	12	31	2	16	,,	,, ,, ,, ,,
19	2	17	38	2	19	48	2	10	,,	,, ,, ,, ,,
20	2	24	58	2	27	00	2	01	,,	,, ,, ,, ,,
21	2	32	26	2	34	35	2	09	,,	,, ,, ,, ,,
22	2	39	52	2	45	26	4	34	,,	No. 4 into pit for fuel and tyre change.
23	2	50	52	2	52	41	1	49	,,	Mercedes Pit for fuel.
24	2	58	14	3	00	00	1	46	,,	Driver of No. 4 Bentley Capt. Woolf Barnato.
25	3	05	32	3	07	15	1	43	,,	,, ,, ,, ,,
26	3	12	51	3	14	32	1	41	,,	,, ,, ,, ,,

Lap	Time Mercedes hr. min. sec.	Time Bentley hr. min. sec.	Lead min. sec.	Leading car	Remarks
27	3 20 08	3 21 47	1 39	Mercedes	Driver of No. 4 Bentley Capt. Woolf Barnato.
28	3 27 30	3 28 56	1 26	,,	,, ,, ,, ,, ,,
29	3 34 45	3 36 09	1 24	,,	,, ,, ,, ,, ,,
30	3 42 10	3 43 22	1 12	,,	,, ,, ,, ,, ,,
31	3 49 32	3 50 41	1 09	,,	,, ,, ,, ,, ,,
32	3 57 03	3 57 51	0 48	,,	,, ,, ,, ,, ,,
33	4 04 34	4 05 05	0 31	,,	,, ,, ,, ,, ,,
34	4 11 54	4 12 11	0 17	,,	,, ,, ,, ,, ,,
35	4 19 15	4 19 23	0 08	,,	,, ,, ,, ,, ,,
36	4 26 36	4 26 34	0 02	Bentley No. 4	,, ,, ,, ,, ,,
37	4 33 41	4 33 52	0 11	Mercedes	,, ,, ,, ,, ,,
38	4 40 50	4 40 56	0 06	,,	,, ,, ,, ,, ,,
39	4 48 00	4 48 02	0 02	,,	,, ,, ,, ,, ,,
40	4 55 17	4 55 10	0 07	Bentley No. 4	,, ,, ,, ,, ,,
41	5 02 31	5 02 28	0 03	,,	,, ,, ,, ,, ,,
42	5 09 44	5 09 45	0 01	Mercedes	,, ,, ,, ,, ,,
43	5 16 55	5 19 37	2 42	,,	No. 4 pit for fuel.
44	5 24 22	5 27 00	2 38	,,	Driver of No. 4 Bentley Com. Glen Kidston, R.N.
45	5 31 50	5 34 42	2 52	,,	,, ,, ,, ,,
46	5 46 14	5 42 12	4 02	Bentley No. 4	Mercedes into pit for fuel.
47	5 53 23	5 49 42	3 41	,,	,, ,, ,, ,, ,,
48	6 00 34	5 57 14	3 20	,,	,, ,, ,, ,, ,,
49	6 07 43	6 04 51	2 52	,,	,, ,, ,, ,, ,,
50	6 14 50	6 12 23	2 29	,,	,, ,, ,, ,, ,,
51	6 22 00	6 19 55	2 05	Bentley No. 4	Mercedes into pit for fuel.
52	6 29 13	6 27 17	1 56	,,	,, ,, ,, ,, ,,
53	6 36 28	6 34 44	1 44	,,	,, ,, ,, ,, ,,
54	6 43 40	6 42 13	1 27	,,	,, ,, ,, ,, ,,

Time

Lap	Mercedes			Bentley			Lead		Leading car	Remarks
	hr.	min.	sec.	hr.	min.	sec.	min.	sec.		
55	6	50	53	6	49	37	1	16	Bentley No. 4	Driver of No. 4 Bentley Com. Glen Kidston, R.N.
56	6	58	03	6	57	06	0	57	,,	,,
57	7	05	09	7	04	37	0	32	,,	,,
58	7	12	10	7	12	06	0	04	,,	,,
59	7	19	13	7	19	29	0	16	Mercedes	,,
60	6	26	24	7	26	55	0	31	,,	,,
61	7	33	40	7	34	18	0	38	,,	,,
62	7	41	05	7	41	39	0	34	,,	,,
63	7	51	05	7	48	57	2	08	Bentley No. 4	Mercedes pit stop.
64	7	59	11	7	56	22	2	49	,,	,,
65	8	06	27	8	07	04	0	37	Mercedes	Bentley in pit for refill.
66	8	13	48	8	14	32	0	44	,,	Driver of No. 4 Bentley Capt. Woolf Barnato.
67	8	21	02	8	22	04	1	02	,,	,,
68	8	31	46	8	29	25	2	21	Bentley No. 4	Mercedes in pit for refill.
69	8	39	40	8	36	55	2	45	,,	,,
70	8	47	43	8	44	27	3	16	,,	,,
71	8	55	37	8	52	03	3	34	,,	,,
72	9	03	36	8	59	33	4	03	,,	,,
73	9	11	37	9	07	27	4	10	,,	,,
74	9	19	18	9	18	10	1	08	,,	Bentley in pit for new tyre.
75	9	27	07	9	25	31	1	36	,,	,,
76	9	34	55	9	32	50	2	05	,,	,,
77	9	42	47	9	40	13	2	34	,,	,,
78	9	50	36	9	47	40	2	56	,,	,,
79	9	58	30	9	55	04	3	26	,,	,,
80	10	06	21	10	02	25	3	56	,,	,,
81	10	41	21	10	09	38	4	43	,,	,,
82	10	22	55	10	17	00	5	55	,,	,,

Mercedes retired—'Battery completely discharged'.

car and trying to pull it off the road with a Bugatti. Just before dark the road is once more clear and we are very relieved.

Since there can be no doubt but that the Bentley No. 4-Mercedes duel for the first half of the race was the incident of predominating interest, an analysis of the time-sheets should prove very helpful to those wishing to form an opinion as regards the relative merits of the two cars.

Let us consider first which car is the faster—regardless of wear, tear and damage to the engine. Caracciola's fastest laps were in the early stages of the race, his second lap being clocked at 7 minutes 1 second and his third in 6 minutes 58 seconds. For these two laps he had a clear course, having got away at the head of the mass, whilst Bentley No. 4 was being held in reserve at this stage of the race, and Glen Kidston, driving to orders, was content to be clocking round about 7 minutes 20 seconds. Tim Birkin, on the other hand, who admittedly was going flat out, and whose run was short but very sweet, put in one lap, his third, at the amazing figure of 6 minutes 48 seconds, giving an average of 89·69 miles per hour for the circuit. No other car clocked under 7 minutes, so that the Mercedes claim to be the fastest production touring car is true, with one exception.

Incidentally, all the sensational rubbish published in the press about elaborate team tactics adopted by the two Bentley groups to 'crack up' the Mercedes are entirely without any foundation in fact. Is it likely that any 'team tactics', however subtle and however brilliant, would direct one of its team to continue racing with a car weighing over $2\frac{1}{4}$ tons at speeds up to 130 m.p.h. on a bare canvas, having thrown the tread two or three miles before the place where the car could have been stopped? Nothing but the individual sheer dare-devilry of our beloved Tim would do this sort of thing. Madness, yes, but rather admirable madness. Tim's driving was brilliant, but very hard on the car—furthermore he never could resist the temptation to play to the gallery in the early stages of a race—if his car survived both these hazards in a long race, as they did, most ably and abetted by the more phlegmatic, but very little slower, Barnato in the 1929 race, he won. How often does one see the chances of a perfect car jeopardized in this way. It is doubtful whether Tim's effort was sufficiently sustained to really affect the Mercedes and this opinion is supported by Caracciola's subsequent regularity, his next fourteen laps after the disappearance of No. 9 showing no more than 5 seconds' variation, being between 7 minutes 15 seconds and 7 minutes 19 seconds. This is not the performance of a 'Pinked Rival'. To return to our time-sheet, it will be observed that Bentley No. 4 lying quietly in reserve during the Birkin-Caracciola duel and later whilst Sammy Davis is gently prodding the Merc in the rear, never being more than 2 minutes 26 seconds behind, and it is not until poor Clive Dunfee's mishap put an end to Bentley No. 3's chances that No. 4 is called up to the front line.

Glen Kidston has played his part admirably, handing over a motor car well placed and in perfect condition to his co-driver, after completing 22 laps. Thanks also to a better-organized pit-stop, by the time the Mercedes and No. 4 get going again 'Babe' is only 1 minute 49 seconds behind.

Having received orders to attack, Babe settles down to a spell of really brilliant driving, clocking the following times: 7·15, 7·19, 7·15, 7·17, 7·15, 7·9, 7·13, 7·13, 7·19, 7·10, 7·14, 7·6, 7·12, 7·11, and by this means having gradually worn away the Mercedes' lead, on the 36th lap we have the joy of seeing No. 4 2 seconds ahead. With the exception of the few minutes that the lead was held by Tim Birkin, before the bursting of his tyre, the Mercedes has led throughout, nearly 4½ hours since flag-fall. Babe is given an enormous reception as he passes the grandstand, for the chase has been a most exciting one for those fans who follow it with their stop-watches. That slow wearing away of the Merc's lead, the very inevitability, like water wearing away the rock, 3 seconds, 3 seconds, 2 seconds, 2, 13, 2, 12, 3, 21, 17, 14, 9, 6, 10, in fact nearer and always nearer until the dramatic moment of passing and triumphantly leading past the stands.

This was a piece of impertinence too great for the Mercedes to tolerate, and thus scattering all thoughts of discretion to the winds, greater demands than ever were made on the supercharger that by increasing his lap speed to 7 minutes 5 seconds, No. 1 came round first with 11 seconds to the good. The next lap was covered in 7·9 and 7·4, respectively thus reducing his lead to 6 seconds. This was followed by a 7·10 and a 7·6, leaving a mere couple of seconds between the two cars. To those of us with previous experience of the Mercedes, it was evident that this sort of thing could only end in one way, for by now the whine of his blower could be heard all round the course. And now the Bentley held the lead for two laps by only 7 and 3 seconds, before coming in for his refill.

By the time both cars had settled down after their refill, the drivers now being Glen Kidston and Werner, the Bentley led by 4 minutes 2 seconds. By means of a spell of brilliant driving, Werner succeeded in wiping out this deficit—considering that the major part of this spell was in the dark, since it did not commence till nearly ten o'clock, the figures are most impressive: 7·9, 7·11, 7·9, 7·7, 7·10, 7·13, 7·15, 7·12, 7·13, 7·10, 7·6, 7·1, 7·3, and at this point on the 59th lap he wrests the lead from Kidston and keeps it till a pit stop 4 laps later. This was probably the most brilliant sustained performance of the whole race, considering it was dark. What a pity the Mercedes pit-work was so poor, necessitating taking so much out of the car in order to make up for it. After the next stops for refill, it was evident that this last effort of No. 1 had been too much for him and that he had shot his bolt, for the Bentley increased a lead of 2·21 to 5·55 in 14 laps, doing the following times: 7·30, 7·35, 7·30, 7·34, 7·54, 7·21, 7·19, 7·23, 7·27, 7·24, 7·21, 7·13, 7·22, and here it was that the Mercedes faded out on lap 82, shortly before 2.30 a.m. on the Sunday morning. The official reason given for the Merc.'s failure was a short in the battery causing a sudden and complete discharge. We are inclined to take this with a grain of salt, having grave suspicions about a gasket!

However satisfactory the result of this duel is to Bentley Motors Ltd., there is no doubt but that the demise of No. 1 has largely taken the interest from the race. Further, Caracciola, Werner and their car have proved themselves most doughty and worthy opponents, possessed of true sportsmanship, ready to give and take knocks inseparable from this kind of competition.

The end of this struggle is the signal for going home, as with the exit of Mercedes it is obvious that Bentleys must win the race. So true is this in actual fact and so far ahead is the Barnato-Kidston Speed-Six that for the last 12 hours of the race it has to do nothing more than a moderately fast tour, to maintain itself in first place.

During the early hours of Sunday morning, the instructions given to Glen Kidston to keep No. 4 rolling round about the 7·45 figure per lap led to a rather amusing incident. Somewhere about midnight, Ramponi had become ill and was not well enough to drive No. 8, so that his partner Benjafield was compelled to take over. Having suffered from repeated tyre trouble during the Saturday afternoon and evening, together with some bother with plugs, Benjafield was four laps behind No. 4. However, since his instructions were to keep going at about 7·20, sooner or later he was bound to overtake and want to pass No. 4. It so happened that he got on to the tail of No. 4 just before Mulsanne and spent most of the succeeding lap in trying to pass it. This Benjafield succeeded in doing only after almost completing another lap by putting the offside two wheels of his car well over the grass verge at a speed in excess of 120 m.p.h. Not expecting to have to do this sort of thing with members of his own team, Benjafield is naturally annoyed and having regained the crown of the road turns round and shakes his fist at Kidston. This is more than Kidston can stand and as No. 8 is braking for Mulsanne, Glen runs up alongside and shouts, 'If you want to hot-stuff me, I can hot-stuff you,' and a bit of a barging match ensues for the corner, which is won by Benjafield, who, naturally incensed with the crass stupidity of it all, vents his wrath on the accelerator pedal, goes crashing through the woods running into the Arnage bends rather more quickly than advisable and thus having to brake correspondingly hard—result, up goes the ump-teenth tread just after the pits, so that nearly a whole lap has to be covered at reduced speed plus the added ignominy of being re-passed by Glen. Some hours later, after No. 8 has finally burst and Benjafield is in the Dorothy Paget *équipe's* pit, Glen Kidston comes down looking quite a bit sheepish and says, 'W.O. has sent me to you to apologize.' Benjafield thanks him and at the same time explains that there was no question of wishing to hot-stuff him or even, being nearly 40 miles astern, of catching him, but it was merely the result of two cars running to scheduled speeds, the speed of the leader being less than the following car. Anyway, explanation being completed, Kidston and Benjafield adjourned for a drink together.

Just before ten o'clock on Sunday morning, Tim comes into the pit with the engine of No. 9 making fearsome explosions. Trouble diagnosed as valves—car withdrawn. Benjafield is not so lucky—his engine blows up with a loud report near Hunaudieres—piston gone—just before 11 a.m. Just as he is about to set out on his long trek back to the pits, having parked the car on the grass verge,

Louis Chiron appears from nowhere with a perfectly good Chrysler Coupé and drives him back. Thank you, Louis! And so with five hours still to go Bentleys are left with two cars in the race out of six entered—certainly these two are lying first and second and look like staying there, but it is woefully short of the standard set last year. However, on analysis it is not so bad, for the supercharged cars are really not out of the experimental stage and for two of them to last as long as they did is most encouraging. Whereas the official works entry, one car only is lost and that not through any mechanical failure.

And so it finished—Nos. 4 and 2, driven by Barnato and Kidston, Clement and Watney, respectively, toured home first and second, Bentley Motors Ltd. having won the race for four years in succession. It was also a colossal personal triumph for Captain Woolf Barnato, Managing Director of the firm, who by winning this race completed his hat-trick. By his performance during his duel with Caracciola he has proved himself one of the best drivers this country has produced.

Although the result of the race is a foregone conclusion many hours before the end, so enthralling is the sheer magnificence of the Bentley performance alone that the crowds return after an early lunch to cheer the victors in no uncertain manner. The cordial generosity of the French is most gratifying and it would have been difficult for them to have shown greater pleasure had they themselves been the winner.

Maybe I have conveyed the impression that this is a match between the two cars alone, if so please allow me to make a correction. Not only were several other cars running, but amongst them were the three other Bentleys whose fate has already been described. Of the rest the two Talbots driven by Lewis and Eaton, Hindmarsh and Rose-Richards, did remarkably well, being most impressive in the regularity of their running, finishing 3rd and 4th respectively, averaging 68 m.p.h. for the 24 hours.

Of the 18 cars that started, 9 finished, qualifying to take part in the race for the seventh Biennial Rudge-Whitworth Cup in the following year. The following is a detailed list:

Car	Driver	Kilo- metres	Miles	Average m.p.h.
1. Bentley	Barnato and Kidston	2930	1821	75·87
2. Bentley	Clement and Watney	2832	1760	73·33
3. Talbot	Lewis and Eaton	2651	1647	68·63
4. Talbot	Hindmarsh and Rose- Richards	2625	1631	67·97
5. Alfa-Romeo	Howe and Callingham	2607	1620	67·50
6. Lea-Francis	Peacock and Newsome	2291	1424	59·33
7. Bugatti	Mmes Mareuse and Siko	2164	1345	56·04
8. Tracta	Gregoire and Vallon	2105	1311	54·62
9. Tracta	Bourcier and Debeugny	2013	1251	52·12

and the result of the

SIXTH BIENNIAL RUDGE-WHITWORTH CUP

		Figure of Merit
1. Bentley	Barnato and Kidston	1172
2. Bentley	Clement and Watney	1133
3. Tracta	Gregoire and Vallon	1054
4. Lea-Francis	Peacock and Newsome	1041
5. Tracta	Bourcier and Debeugny	1009

As we said good-bye the following morning to all our good friends we of the Hon Dorothy Paget *équipe* basking in some of the glory reflected from the works team, and pretending to be all of the victorious team, little did any of us think that 1930 was the last time Bentley Motors Ltd. would compete at Le Mans. Of course we knew that the company had weathered several financial crises in the past, but never in our blackest moods had we ever considered the possibility of the complete eclipse of the company that had produced these wonderful cars, for the sake of a few thousand pounds. Surely such a car was a national asset, an asset sufficiently valuable to be subsidized by the state rather than that it should be permitted to be swamped by some financial jiggery-pokery.

From *The Bentleys at Le Mans*
by J. D. Benjafield, 1948, and
reproduced by permission.

Appendix Two

In the course of work on this book I had to look through a number of old volumes of *The Autocar*, and re-read with interest the road tests of several of the cars for which I was responsible. I thought it might be useful to reproduce one or two of these here to give some idea of what people thought of the cars at the time they were first produced. The first of these is a most kindly and tolerant one, considering what a rough-and-ready prototype he had to contend with, by S. C. H. 'Sammy' Davis; and also shows, incidentally, that the road tests by the motoring press in those days were perhaps rather less exacting than they are today. The second, of the big 8-litre car, as well as making some curious passing criticism of our sales people, does emphasize something that is easily forgotten about this short-lived car —namely its sheer performance. The 8-litre, in spite of its great size and weight, was faster in almost all respects than both the Speed Six and the supercharged 4½-litre cars; for example it took only 7 seconds, against 7½ for the Six and 10½ for the S/C 4½, to accelerate from 10 to 30 m.p.h. in top gear; and with 42 seconds from 10 to 90 m.p.h. in top, was 8 seconds faster than the S/C 4½ and 19 seconds faster than the Speed Six. Its top speed was faster than both cars, too.

The report on the V12 Lagonda speaks for itself, and makes me more than ever sorry that the opportunity never arose to develop that car further.

From The Autocar *January 24th 1920*

A TEST OF A 3-LITRE BENTLEY

A car which combines Docility in Traffic with Exceptional Speed Potentiality on the Open Road

Although frowned upon by the authorities, limited by law and penalized when discovered, speed is the greatest attribute of a car, and from the car alone is it possible to realize to the full that peculiar feeling of greatness, soaring almost to poetic heights, consequent on high-speed travelling.

There are, however, certain private roads in our own country, and nearly all the national highways of fair France, on which a racing machine and an open throttle are not only allowed, but encouraged, to the great joy and thankfulness of those drivers who know really where the true pleasure of motoring exists.

Quite recently we were enabled to make a trial of the 3-litre Bentley, a car designed to give a great speed, yet to remain tractable and docile in the hands of an unskilled owner and to be suitable also for Britain with British road conditions. The machine is one just completed, untuned, unaltered and hand-built, with a rough, four-seated body carrying the mud of previous runs, lacking a hood, with a narrow windscreen—in fact, having bare accommodation for four people. Not very handsome to look upon (test bodies seldom are), not altogether free from straps and string, the car bore an air of something indefinable, just a suggestion, perhaps, of what was to come, a knowledge, maybe, of its own power; at all events, something which showed its breed through the external work-a-day disguise.

Cars undoubtedly have a personality to the real enthusiast, to whom they are not mere collections of steel and aluminium, but, animal-like, show their spirit just so soon as the clutch bites home and feeling comes to the driver through the narrow steel steering-wheel rim.

Our start was typical; the engine, responding at once to the electric motor, emitted a steady roar from the exhaust; the crew, well wrapped up, soon settled down to comfort in their seats, and, with one or two of those little dabs at the throttle beloved by all Brooklands drivers, the car moved off.

For the first part of the journey we travelled as steadily as could be wished over bad roads, betraying little of the engine's power, save when an occasional opportunity demanded rapid acceleration; the general behaviour of the chassis suggested an entire absence of effort combined with more than ordinary tractability, the power of either brake being something altogether extraordinary and impossible to believe, save from the evidence of actual experience.

THE ENGINE'S FULL SONG

All this was done with the air of a lithe, active and speedy animal straining a little on the leash. Presently a long stretch of familiar road, quite deserted, with a lining of trees, unrolled ahead. Each member of the crew, as if by instinct, settled farther down into the seat, drew in a deep breath, and inwardly said, 'Now!' Instantly the exhaust changed its note from a purr to a most menacing roar, the white ribbon of road streamed towards the car, while the backs of the seats pressed hard upon one's shoulder blades.

As the speed increased to over 70 m.p.h. the landscape leaped at us, wind shrieked past the screen, while the flanking trees and other objects seemed, not definitely and sharply contoured, but a blurred streak hurtling past as the roar of the exhaust rose to its full song. To such an accompaniment the pulse beats quicker, there comes an almost irresistible desire to burst into some wild war song, greater even than the immortal song of Roland—in defiance of the demons that howl invisible without. Every part of one's being urges greater speed in the fierce wild intoxication of a moment supreme above all others in the life sensations of man. A curve flashes past with just the suggestion of altered course, mayhap with a small shower of stones slung up from behind, but still the silver radiator rushed towards that dark unattainable line of the horizon, which seems so near yet never is attained.

BRAKES A PREDOMINANT FEATURE

Then the throttle comes back, abruptly the noise dies down, and the brakes take a hold upon the drums as all one's exaltation dies, leaving a curious sense of shame, as though for a moment one's soul had been exposed to the rude, not to say unsympathetic, gaze of other men.

But those fierce few minutes are worth much as a memory, even more than similar experience on the Big Benz or a low-flying aeroplane, for the Bentley is but a small machine by comparison.

The reader may say, 'This is all very well, but what of the car?' Well, the best description of this car is one of its speed; for the rest, the brakes are the most predominant feature. Smoothly and without chatter, they draw the car up in an altogether incredibly short distance—so short, indeed, that one is still bracing for the smash when the car stops dead many yards from the obstacle.

RACER AND TOWN CARRIAGE COMBINED

There are, of course, numberless small things of note. The gears of the double oil-pump drive are noisy, somewhere in the engine something emits a peculiar penetrating grate every now and again, while much good oil is sprayed over the engine by the breather pipes. These are faults inseparable from the first chassis of a new design, are easily overcome and are no impediment to success.

The car holds the road all square, corners admirably and is well sprung. In England, as a short run proved, the machine can travel without protest, chatter or difficulty on top gear at 10 m.p.h. or under, can pick up from that to high speed, or take a hill slowly and easily; in fact, the 3-litre Bentley—racer on occasion though it may be—is endowed with all the desired features for town carriage work of the most docile type.

For the man who wants a true sporting type of light-bodied car for use on a Continental tour—where speed limits are not meant to be observed, unless one is involved in an accident—the 3-litre Bentley is undoubtedly the car *par excellence.* Its comparatively small size renders it an extraordinarily easy car to handle, not only on the open road, but also in congested city streets.

From The Autocar, *December 5th, 1930*

8-LITRE BENTLEY SALOON

MOTORING IN ITS VERY HIGHEST FORM:
THE TREMENDOUS PERFORMANCE

It may seem slightly unusual to commence a description of a car's test by disagreeing quite thoroughly with a statement made by a representative of the manufacturer when introducing the model at one of the firm's functions, but so great appears to be the discrepancy between what one would naturally expect and what is actually provided that a word or two of argument is essential.

At the time of the Olympia Show the 8-litre Bentley was introduced in such a way as to stress to the full the fact that it was designed to be that rather mysterious type of vehicle which is generally known as a town carriage; and undoubtedly a great many people who listened to that announcement went away under the impression that performance was the very last thing on which the car based its claim to consideration—so much so that certain people undoubtedly believed that the performance was sacrificed to obtain other possibilities.

Now, in the first place, although everybody knows what is meant by a town carriage, and, further, can realize the distinction between that and a sports car, it is not, in fact, easy to see where one type stops and the other begins. Quite apart from that, the one thing, the dominant note, of the new Bentley is its tremendous performance, and on that performance alone it stands right in the forefront as an equal, at least, of any other car in existence. One glance at the figures shows, as no sentences or phrasing can, that the big 8-litre is something out of the common run, even when allowances are made for the increase in engine capacity as compared with the 6½ litres of the earlier six-cylinder model.

Therefore, it is impossible to allow that the car can be described, or in any way regarded, as just a town carriage and nothing more; and to remain silent concerning, or in any way belittle, the performance factor is, from the sales point of view, to disregard the principal reason why this splendid car should succeed.

Had it been that the performance made the car difficult to handle on top gear at low speed, heavy to manœuvre in traffic or in a confined space, harsh or noisy, then the performance by itself might justly be regarded as simply that of a sports car, though few of these features are easily noticeable even in the modern sports car, unless it has been tuned for racing.

Quite on the contrary, this car can be driven really softly on its high top gear as slowly as a man walks, and can accelerate from that without snatch and without difficulty, and the whole time the engine, being well within its power, is silent and smooth; in fact, it is only really apparent that there is a big engine working under the bonnet at all, and that so high a top ratio is used, when the machine is accelerated from a crawl. For all practical purposes, therefore, the machine does its work on the one gear, in town or out of it, and it is with that one gear that it best suits the average driver.

The new gearbox is interesting, the longer movement of the lever from one slot to another being a little puzzling at first to any-one who is accustomed to the earlier models, a point emphasized because to start on second and then change at once to top is the obvious way of handling the machine. The gears are quieter than before, and will be quieter still when there has been opportunity to obtain more experience with this type of box.

The use of two broad shoes in each of the rear-wheel brake drums, instead of four relatively narrow shoes, has certainly im-proved the brake power, and certain alterations have made the vacuum servo motor seem more definite and more positive, so that to the driver it really appears as though he can feel the shoes touch the drums and thus command a more delicate control. But the great change in the machine, apart from its engine, is the way in which the car, travelling fast and with a saloon body, can be taken round curves and corners with its shock absorbers adjusted as for town work. It is true that when once one was accustomed to the earlier 6½-litre that model seemed as steady as could be wished—provided the shock absorbers were really tight—yet the new car is steady with easy riding springs and so puts the earlier model entirely in the shade, a thing due in great part to the big, stiff frame, though the fact that the springs are farther apart and the chassis lower may have a great deal to do with it as well; and this rigidity makes the big car almost as tractable as one of the smallest machines on the road, while it seems to have no side sway whatsoever on a fast corner.

It is possible, of course, to go right over the chassis, pointing out here and there where improvement is apparent, but, when all is said, it is not a matter of detail improvement that makes the 8-litre Bentley what it is, for the thing that counts above everything else is the way in which the big machine does its work, and its great sense of latent power. Exactly this and nothing else is the real reason why so big a machine has a future.

Putting it another way, one can breakfast comfortably in London yet lunch at Catterick Bridge, and during the whole of a run of this type there was none of the intenseness that usually comes into fast driving; indeed, it was practically impossible to believe that the car was travelling at anything like the pace the speedometer showed, though subsequent tests showed that speedometer to be reasonably accurate. In spite of the average, not a single village or town was traversed at anything like the pace that is maintained by the driver of an ordinary car, and in most cases it seemed much more pleasant to go through at a genuine 11 to 15 m.p.h.

Apart from that, the best testimonial to the ease with which the car did its work lay in the fact that the occupants of the two front seats were conversing naturally during the whole of the run.

In France the Bentley has kept up a cruising speed of 70 m.p.h. without the engine seeming to do anything at all, and, if the long northern roads offer, can go right up to 100 m.p.h. on the flat with surprisingly little apparent effort.

PERFORMANCE FIGURES

Acceleration	10–30 m.p.h.	4-2/5 secs.
Maximum speed	101·12 m.p.h.	
Weight	48 cwt. 0 qr. 14 lb.	

From The Autocar, *March 11th, 1938*

42-H.P. TWELVE-CYLINDER LAGONDA SALOON

When a renowned designer and his associates—in this instance
W. O. Bentley and his technical staff—set themselves the task of
evolving a car which shall rank in the very forefront of machines
produced today, and have the backing of capital and modern works
resources, it would only be a matter of surprise if that car failed to
be outstanding. This is an impression of the atmosphere in which
the twelve-cylinder Lagonda has been created.

Well over a year ago the car was first heard of publicly. The
interval has been devoted to developing it from the early stages of
an entirely new design to the point of production; and the waiting
has been worth while to those who appreciate a fine car. It is a
magnificent machine.

Opinion can be based upon the experiences of a particularly
comprehensive test run, over several days, in which a wide variety
of roads was covered, making up a total distance of more than
700 miles. Much can be conveyed by the bare comment that every
one of those seven hundred miles was a delight. High opinion has
been formed of the car as a whole, even from the standpoint that
has to be taken, namely that it costs some £1500, and therefore
should be superlative.

It is the short chassis version that has been tried, and this
example represents the first of these cars with final-drive ratio now
adopted, and other modifications incorporated, to undergo im-
partial test.

Somehow it seems almost an insult to so remarkable a car to
take it feature by feature, and appraise each of them in the usual
manner. It is as an entity that such a car stands or falls. Each major
item of engine, chassis, and body must do its proper share in making
up the car de luxe, and none be disproportionately prominent at
the expense of others.

This desirable state of affairs has been achieved. The aim of
those responsible was not to produce a car having sheer speed as
its be all and end all, but one that should be naturally and easily
capable of 100 m.p.h. at least, by reason of its engine design, and
gearing, and provide really comfortable travel on the road.

Let these claims be examined in the light of unbiased experience.

As to performance, the Lagonda shows itself able to go up to well over the 100; its acceleration is tremendous. As to comfort, driver and passengers can sit in it all day and yet not wish for a change of position, and regular passengers comment that they cannot remember travelling in a car less affected by road surface or one in which even extremely fast cornering is as little apparent, so exceptionally does it remain level and steady, so slight is the evidence of mechanism working.

PASSENGER DOZING AT 100 M.P.H.

Vivid illustration comes from an actual instance during this test, when more than 60 m.p.h. had been averaged over a certain section of safe open road, devoid of hedges or obscured crossings, and the 100 reading had been shown, yet a back-seat passenger dozed meanwhile. There is no sense of strain upon the human factor, and it scarcely seems possible that the speed should be as high as is indicated.

Few roads in this country permit such motoring. Not always does one want it, of course; but as a result of there being so much in reserve, the Lagonda runs at speeds between 70 and 80 m.p.h. as good smaller cars do at 50 or 60. The most practical appeal of the car lies in the manner in which it wafts along at a small throttle opening and low revs, disdaining gradient, overtaking in a clean sweep with an extra touch of throttle, and ready to soar to the eighties and nineties wherever there is a chance and the driver wills. It is a wonderful motoring experience to see the speedometer needle at 90 up a long slope of the kind found on roads across Salisbury Plain and in parts of Dorset.

EASILY ACHIEVED HIGH PERFORMANCE

Performance is apt to be stressed. It is a great part of the car, but the merit of the sheer test figures, outstanding as these are as a set, is increased by the fact of their being obtained without apparently over-stressing the engine or making it noisy or rough.

On the other side of things, it is a docile, easily handled car, just as well able to fit in with the leisurely mood of driving. It can be moved off gently on second gear and top put in within a few yards, and it will creep about on top gear, accelerating smoothly from a crawl. When picking up from the lower speeds some slight pinking is evident; there is no hand ignition lever, the control being automatic in the two distributors.

In top gear the comfortable non-snatch minimum is 6–7 m.p.h., and the engine shows a fine capacity to pull against gradient at low speeds without a change down being necessary, though here may be mentioned a striking point peculiar to the new twelve-cylinder Lagonda among production engines of considerable size. It is capable of much higher crankshaft speeds than has been general practice with this size of engine. The red warning light on the rev counter is set at 5500 r.p.m., and up to 5000 at any rate, is an everyday usable figure on the indirects if a driver should be so inclined. Thus the maxima on the gears are exceptionally high, and it can become a 'gearbox' car, greatly adding to the interest on occasion. Yet at the same time the engine has top-gear flexibility.

In considering the exceptional performance, it must be remembered that the V-type engine is of no more than 4½-litre capacity. The speedometer on this particular car displayed the unusual trait of becoming slower in its readings as the speed rose. being almost dead accurate at 10, 20 and 30, but 1 m.p.h. slow at 60 and 80, and showing the highest reading of only 98–99 when the car was timed at 103·45 m.p.h. This was at 5200 r.p.m. but, if conditions permit, the engine can go on increasing revs usefully, the power peak not having been reached. A lap at Brooklands track was covered at 97·95 m.p.h. Wind conditions were not helpful, though not adverse. Another interesting point is that in a quarter-mile, using the gears, a speed of 73 m.p.h. was attained.

For the gear change the best type of synchromesh is used on second, third and top, the lever being rigid and moving with a pleasing positiveness into each gear. The drop to first remains a plain double-declutching change, but is likely to be needed very seldom indeed, to judge by behaviour on steep and narrow hills of considerable gradient in the West Country, where there was all the power that could be wanted in second gear. Both second and third are so quiet running as to be unnoticed, and it is possible at some speeds for the driver to forget to change to third and find that it is already engaged.

The brakes, hydraulically operated through twin master cylinders, make the driving of this car a safe and confident procedure, and that is really all that need be said of them, though the exceptionally light operation must be mentioned. As might be expected, the steering is not low geared (3½ turns from lock to lock), and a most satisfactory balance has been achieved. It gives the essential accuracy of control up at the top speeds, with no trace of road-wheel movement, and is not heavy to turn when the car is nearly stationary. The clutch action, again, is particularly light, and the whole control and 'feel' of the car are completely different from what may have been associated with Lagondas of some years ago.

INDEPENDENT SPRINGING ADVANTAGES

Unquestionably, the independent front-wheel springing—in which a system of long torsion bars carried in the frame members is used —gives not only the comfort of riding already emphasized, but also shock-free steering and an almost uncanny degree of road-holding. The driver comes up to a corner fast, turns the wheel, and the car goes round, with no after effects. There is no more than that in the process.

As to the driving position points, particularly at first a shallow windscreen is noticed, but both wings are visible. The steering wheel is on the high side; the column is adjustable, and was not at its lowest setting. The handbrake lever is in an ideal position, lying horizontally to the right of the driving seat, and is of the fly-off type, proving dead-sure for holding the car on a hill. When the driver is wearing gloves, it is found to be a little too close to the seat cushion.

The placing of the central lever renders use of the near-side door awkward if the driving seat is adjusted well forward. For some reason, possibly the fact of the wings projecting beyond the point where the driver can actually see them, it proved a not altogether easy car to manœuvre at low speed in a tight space, though actually it is relatively compact.

There are some details applying to the car that has been tried which have since received attention for production. The main instrument lighting certainly needs improving; the dials are particularly clear by daylight, and the speedometer and rev counter needles of the 'dead-beat' type. Again, the foot-operated anti-dazzle switch could be more convenient. The head-lamp beam allows almost full speed at night, which says enough.

Exterior lines have been slightly changed in the latest cars, the striking fairing of the front wings becoming less accentuated. The front seat back-rests are adjustable for angle, which is a valuable point. There are two external mirrors which, adjusted to suit a given driving position, give a good view behind, except directly astern.

NEAT ENGINE

Considering what it comprises, the engine is neat. At least four sparking plugs look awkward to reach; the oil filler is well placed but the dipstick could be easier to withdraw. One of the S.U. carburettors has combined with it a thermostatically regulated auxiliary starting carburettor, no hand-mixture control being fitted; the engine fires at once, and pulls almost immediately from cold. Water temperature is observed to run low.

In a dummy spare wheel cover on the near side is the whole tool kit, as well as the operating mechanism for the hydraulic jacks, The luggage compartment in the tail is of good but not exceptional capacity. Duplicated petrol fillers are a practical point, and all fillers have quick-acting caps.

PERFORMANCE FIGURES

0–30 m.p.h. through gears	4·0 sec.
0–50 ,, ,, ,,	9·7 ,,
0–60 ,, ,, ,,	12·9 ,,
0–70 ,, ,, ,,	17·9 ,,
Maximum on gears 1st	32 m.p.h.
,, ,, ,, 2nd	63 ,,
,, ,, ,, 3rd	86 ,,
,, ,, ,, Top	103·45 m.p.h.

Weight, without passenger, 39 cwt. 2 qr. 14 lb.

Index